SOUND INNOVATIONS
for **GUITAR**

A Revolutionary Method for Individual or Class Instruction

Aaron **STANG** | Bill **PURSE**

How to Use This Book

This book contains 36 complete lesson plans directly correlated to *Sound Innovations for Guitar Book 1*. For high school-age students we project that each lesson will take about a week to complete. Younger students may take longer. How much time is devoted to each lesson plan is at your discretion.

Each unit features goals, National Standards addressed, a full step-by-step lesson plan broken into multiple sections, observational assessments, suggested expansion material, additional advice, and guidance as to expected outcomes. The last lesson of each level is a review and formal assessment unit that is used to reinforce what's been covered and to assess student progress. These lessons should be used in conjunction with the DVD and MP3 examples. It is critical for students to listen closely to all the music examples before attempting to play them, and the videos provide excellent up-close technique demonstrations. Additional resources

such as free reproducible worksheets are available online and are cited throughout the lesson plans.

We assume that if you're teaching guitar, you have a background in music, however, we don't assume that you have a background in guitar. Different teachers will use the student and teacher editions in different ways, but this approach ensures that any school band director or classroom music teacher can provide a class with the foundation students need to pursue guitar at higher levels.

Finally, a note on the multimedia aspects of *Sound Innovations for Guitar*: this teacher edition does not come with the DVD and MP3 discs that are included in the student book. So we recommend that you have your own copy of the student book. Having both the student and teacher editions as you instruct the class, along with the media components, will ensure seamless application of the method as you lead students into the world of guitar.

How to Use the DVD Provided with the Student Book

For video components: When inserted into a DVD player, the DVD will functional as a typical DVD. A chapter menu will open allowing you direct access to over 40 DVD chapters and special features. When inserted into the DVD-ROM drive of a computer, your DVD player software should open, allowing the disc to function as a standard DVD.

For the SI Player: It's recommended that you install the SI Player to your computer so you can use it without the disc. Once the SI Player is installed, you will be able to use all of its functions—it will access all the MP3 files and allow you to slow them down, loop them, and even change keys.

On a PC, close the DVD player and double click on the DVD-ROM drive, which will open to reveal multiple folders inside. Copy both the "SI Player" and "SoundInnovations-Guitar-MP3s" folders to your Desktop. Make sure

both folders end up in the same location. From there you can open the "SI_Player_For_Guitar.exe" file to run the SI Player.

On a Mac, close the DVD player and double click on the DVD-ROM drive. Open the "SI Player" folder and double-click the "SI Player for Guitar" install package. The installer will prompt you through the rest of the process.

For the audio components: Double click on the DVD-ROM drive. The "SoundInnovations-Guitar-MP3s" folder contains all the MP3 files. You can either play the MP3s directly from there or drag them into your music player, such as iTunes.

Cover guitar photos:
Fender Custom Shop Thinline Telecaster courtesy Fender Musical Instruments
Robert Ruck Classic Guitar courtesy Aaron Stang
Duesenberg Starplayer GTV courtesy of Duesenberg USA
Taylor 614 courtesy of Taylor Guitars
Martin D28 courtesy of Martin Guitars
PRS Santana Model courtesy PRS Guitars

© 2012 Alfred Music Publishing Co., Inc.
Sound Innovations™ is a trademark of Alfred Music Publishing Co., Inc.
All Rights Reserved including Public Performance

ISBN-10: 0-7390-9043-7 ISBN-13: 978-0-7390-9043-5

LEVEL 5

LEVEL 6

APPENDIX 1

APPENDIX 2

APPENDIX 3

LESSON 1 | Notes on the 6th String and First Chords

GOALS	• Learn low E, F, and G; ledger lines; quarter notes and half notes; and rhythm slash notation. • Play simple bass line examples with correct rhythm and strum first chords (E, F Flamenco, and G Flamenco). • Explore Flamenco music.
NATIONAL STANDARDS	NS2 (Playing), NS5 (Reading), NS6 (Listening), NS8 (Making Connections), NS9 (History & Culture)

LESSON 1A (First Notes, Page 4)

1. DVD chapter 2 introduces the first notes. Students should always view the DVD chapters before learning new material and then use them as a review resource.

   Note *If you are using the* Sound Innovations *DVD in a computer or DVD player that has the option of using titles or chapters, make sure it is set to chapters to follow the DVD chapter numbers in the* Sound Innovations *guitar method.*

   a. Demonstrate and describe the low E, F, and G notes. Call out the notes and have students play as requested. Students should play and say the notes together out loud. Circulate throughout the class checking hand position and fingering, assisting with any difficulties.

   b. Describe and explain ledger lines. (See Worksheet #1, available as a free, reproducible document online at www.alfred.com/SoundInnovations/SIGuitar.)

2. Line 2: "First Notes." Perform line 2 with students. Make sure to use divided counting throughout.

3. Lines 3–4: Students should break into small groups of two to four each to practice and perform lines 3 and 4. Students can also play along with MP3 tracks 2–4. Go from group to group assisting as needed.

OBSERVATIONAL ASSESSMENTS

- Left hand: Fingers curved, playing on fingertips. Fingers do not interfere with adjacent strings. Thumb centered behind neck.
- Right hand: Pick is held between thumb and index finger, hand is relaxed, and all notes are played with a down-stroke of the pick: pick strikes the string with a downward attack, towards the floor, coming to rest on the 5th string.
- Rhythm: Notes should be played with a steady beat.

LESSON 1B (First Chords, Page 5)

1. DVD chapter 3 introduces the E, F Flamenco, and G Flamenco chords.

2. Lines 5 and 6: Demonstrate and describe the E chord. Listen to MP3 track 6 then ask students to perform line 6. Circulate throughout the class checking hand position and fingering and assisting with any difficulties.

3. Line 7: "Moving Chords." Play MP3 track 7 before asking students to perform. Always let students hear the corresponding MP3 tracks before they attempt to play. We want them to know how their songs should

sound **before** they play. Demonstrate moving the E chord shape up one fret to play F Flamenco and then releasing all strings to play the G Flamenco chord (all demonstrated on DVD chapter 3). Students should retain the "E grip" so they can easily land back on F Flamenco. Ask students to perform line 7. Circulate throughout the class checking hand position and fingering, assisting with any difficulties.

4. Line 8: "Flamenco Mood." This is the students' first opportunity to perform a real duet. Watch DVD chapter 4 first (or listen to MP3 track 8). Ask students to break into groups and begin practicing line 8, "Flamenco Mood." Important: All students should learn and perform both the guitar 1 and guitar 2 parts.

OBSERVATIONAL ASSESSMENTS

- When playing the E chord, fingers should be curved and not interfering with, or muting, adjacent strings. Ask students to hold the E chord and play one string at a time. All six strings should ring clearly. Same is true for all chords.
- Ask students to slide the E shape up one fret to F Flamenco. Fingers should move in perfect tandem—the "E grip" just slides up the neck.
- All duets should be in time with a solid beat.
- As students gain confidence suggest they add variety and interest by playing louder and softer, explore slower and faster tempos, etc.

SOUND ADVICE

- To reinforce music literacy and ledger lines, print and distribute Worksheet #1 from www.alfred.com/SoundInnovations/SIGuitar.
- Discuss and research Flamenco music as described on the next page.

FLAMENCO MUSIC

Flamenco music is an exciting and often virtuosic showcase for the guitarist. This style of guitar playing originated in Andalusia, a region in Spain. Flamenco is actually the native folk music of the Andalusia Gypsies from southern Spain. Flamenco style combines song and dance and the Flamenco musicians often grow up totally immersed in the culture, coming from generations of Flamenco dancers and musicians.

Flamenco guitarists use a nylon string guitar, similar to a classical guitar but unique to their style of music. The strings on a Flamenco guitar are usually very close to the fingerboard making it easier to play the lightning-quick runs associated with this style. Also, the guitars are made of cypress and spruce, giving them a much brighter sound than the classical guitar. The guitars usually have violin-style tuning keys, instead of modern tuners with metal gears, and they have plastic tap-plates on the top of the guitar. Flamenco guitarists often tap out percussion parts and loud accents on these tap plates with their fingernails.

INNOVATIONS @HOME

Ask the class to research Flamenco music on the Internet. Find videos and audio recordings of Flamenco guitar performances. A brief paper can be assigned asking students to research and report on Flamenco music or one of its great performers.

SOUND ADVICE

To reinforce chord fingerings and playing chords in rhythm, print and distribute Worksheet #2, "Making the Changes," from www.alfred.com/SoundInnovations/SIGuitar.

SOUND EXPECTATIONS

- Reasonable expectations based on understanding long- and short-term goals are critical to student success and maintaining appropriate assessments. For each lesson in the book we will provide guidance as to reasonable expectations for student progress.

- Lines 2–4 are reasonably simple single-note exercises using the first three notes. Within the first week students should be able to read and perform these examples with a fair degree of note accuracy and steady rhythm.

- Assist students with left hand position and technique: thumb behind neck, fingers arched, fingertips perpendicular to the fretboard and not interfering with other strings.

- Assist students with right hand position and technique: elbow rests on top of guitar, wrist is arched away from the guitar, pick is held loosely between the thumb and index finger, all notes are played with a down-stroke of the pick, the pick should briefly come to rest on the 5th string after passing though the note on the 6th string.

- Lines 5–8 revolve around the E, F Flamenco, and G Flamenco chords. After the first week, students should have each of the chords memorized and not need to reference the book. They should be able to play each chord; however, some will not be able to change chords while maintaining a steady rhythm and some will not be able to play each chord cleanly without accidentally muting strings. **Playing chords accurately, grabbing them as fast as needed and then being able to strum and change chords with a steady rhythm are long-term goals.** It would not be reasonable to expect most students to perform lines 7 or 8 perfectly at this time. However, the great news is that guitarists can play countless songs with a handful of chords. The same chords and patterns arise in song after song and that is how the guitarist gains mastery— through repetition over time.

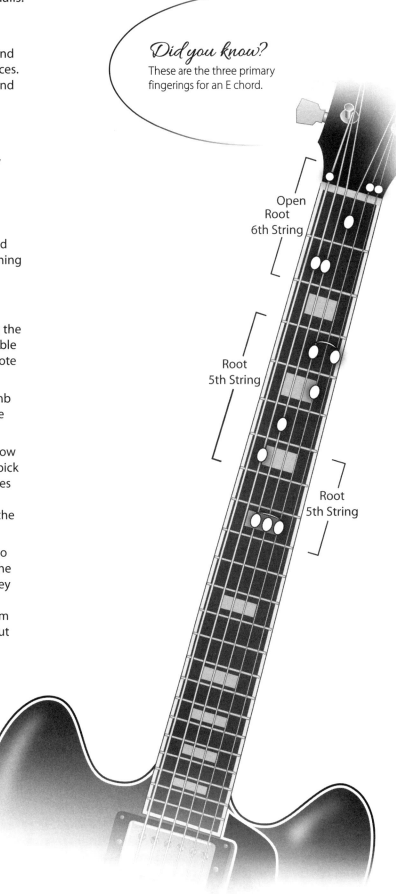

Did you know?
These are the three primary fingerings for an E chord.

Open
Root
6th String

Root
5th String

Root
5th String

LESSON 2 | Notes on the 5th String and the Am Chord

GOALS
- Learn the 5th string notes A, B, and C; reinforce ledger lines, quarter notes, and eighth notes; and learn the musical terms etude and fermata.
- Play simple melody and bass line examples with correct rhythm, strum E, F Flamenco, and Am chords.
- Explore rock and blues music styles.

NATIONAL STANDARDS NS2 (Playing), NS5 (Reading), NS6 (Listening), NS8 (Making Connections)

LESSON 2A (5th String Notes, Page 6)

1. Sound Check: Check tuning with the MP3 tuning track or use electronic tuner.

2. DVD chapter 5 introduces the 5th string notes as does MP3 track 9.

3. Demonstrate and describe the 5th string low A, B, and C. Call out the notes and ask students to play as requested. Students should play and say the notes together out loud.

   Note *When setting up the guitar classroom make sure you have enough room between each student's chair to circulate throughout the class to check hand position and assist with any difficulties.*

   Review technique: Fingers directly behind the fret. Are notes clear? If buzzing, is the fingertip directly behind the fret? Keep in mind there is a point where adding left-hand pressure does not improve the sound. Discovering this balance in technique is what the student should listen for during his or her classroom or practice room performances.

4. Review all of the bass ledger lines with the class. Worksheet #3 (Note Speller, Strings 5 and 6) can be reproduced and assigned as either an in-class or take-home assessment. It is available as a free, reproducible document at www.alfred.com/SoundInnovations/SIGuitar.

   Note *By learning notes starting from the 6th string towards the 1st, we are progressing up the musical alphabet. Make sure the students know that this musical alphabet is A, B, C, D, E, F, G, and repeats. There is an important additional benefit of learning the notes on the 6th and 5th strings—that is where root notes for the standard guitar chords are located.*

5. Line 10: "New Notes." Have the students focus on divided counting ("1 and 2 and 3 and 4 and"). Play MP3 track 10 and ask students to play along. Observe and assist as needed.

6. Line 11, "Stay Down." Play MP3 track 11 and ask the class to play along. Once this line is familiar have the students play and say the letter names at the same time.

   Note *Demonstrate to the class how to use the SI Player using track 11. It is important that the class understands the simple controls for track selection, volume, slowing down the tracks, and looping. Stress to the students that there is always a tempo where he or she can play the exercise or song without errors.* ***It is important that they are practicing correctly and performing the music, not practicing mistakes.***

7. Distribute Worksheet #4 (blank staff and tablature).

   a. Demonstrate how to draw a treble clef (G clef) and have the students practice on their manuscript paper.

   b. Discuss the three components of a written note: notehead, stem, and flag or beam. Demonstrate the proper way to write notes on the staff. Ask the class to practice this notation technique.

   c. Demonstrate how the final bar line is a double bar with a heavy second line.

   d. Ask the class to copy "Still Stay Down" as written in the staff, adding the bar lines as needed. Students need to make sure the stems are going in the correct direction.

   e. Next, students can write the fret numbers on the proper strings of the tablature staff. (0 = open note, 1 = 1st fret, 2 = 2nd fret, 3 = 3rd fret, and 4 = 4th fret.) Remember, the numbers on the tablature staff are fret locations, not fingerings.

8. Line 12: "Eighth Note Etude." Listen to MP3 track 12, then perform the song with the students. Utilize divided counting throughout. Use the SI Player to adjust the track to a tempo the entire class can accurately play. It is helpful to take this etude one measure at a time. Once a measure is familiar, have the students play and say the letter names at the same time.

9. Students can break into small groups to practice and perform Line 12. Go from group to group assisting as needed. Also, this etude is a great warm-up that can be used at the start of each class or practice session.

OBSERVATIONAL ASSESSMENTS

- Left hand: Fingers curved, playing on fingertips. Fingers do not interfere with adjacent strings. Thumb centered behind neck.

- Right hand: Pick is held between thumb and index finger, hand is relaxed, and all notes are played with a down-stroke of the pick, in which the pick strikes the string with a downward attack, towards the floor, coming to rest on the 4th string.

- Rhythm: Notes should be played with a steady beat.

- Notation of symbols, pitches, and rhythms are properly written to manuscript paper.

LESSON 2B (The A Minor Chord, Page 7)

1. DVD chapter 6 introduces the Am chord.

2. Demonstrate and describe the Am chord. Point out that by simply moving the E chord shape down one set of strings towards the floor they will have the Am chord. Listen to MP3 track 13 then ask students to play the chord.

> **Note** *Visualization and chord memory can be reinforced by having the student work away from the guitar using Worksheet #5 to write the chords they are currently using. Have them picture the chord in the mind's eye then write it down.*

3. Line 14: "A Minor Ensemble." DVD chapter 7 and MP3 track 14 both demonstrate this song. Always let students listen and watch before they attempt to play. Important: All students should learn and perform both the Guitar 1 and Guitar 2 parts.

4. Line 15: "Driving Rhythm."

   a. Play MP3 track 15. Students should listen to both guitar parts. All students should learn and perform both guitar parts.

   b. Explain the term fermata as defined in the student book and demonstrate. Divide the class in half and have one section play Guitar 1 and the other Guitar 2. Conduct the performance and have the class watch you for the fermata, then have the class cut off the final note and chord together by touching the right-hand palm to the strings close to the bridge.

   c. Switch parts. Ask the students to practice at a tempo, set with the SI Player, at which they can play with no, or minimal, mistakes. Ask students to break into small groups and begin practicing.

> **Note** *As an alternative to using the MP3 tracks, it is valuable and fun to have a drum beat going with the rock and blues examples being played in class. A basic drum loop from such music production software as GarageBand will help the students feel the beat and lock into a steady tempo.*

OBSERVATIONAL ASSESSMENTS

- When playing the Am chord, fingers should be curved and not interfering with, or muting, adjacent strings. Ask students to hold the Am chord and play one string at a time. The bottom five strings should ring clearly. The same is true for all chords.

- All duets should be in time with a solid beat.

- As students gain confidence suggest they add variety and interest by playing louder and softer, exploring slower and faster tempos, etc.

SOUND ADVICE

"I just go where the guitar takes me."

— ANGUS YOUNG

- Ask students to move the Am shape up one set of strings towards the ceiling to form the E chord. Fingers should move over in perfect tandem—the "E grip" moves as a unit not one finger at a time. Ask the class to repeatedly play E to Am.

- Distribute suggested worksheets (Worksheets 4 and 5) from this lesson.

- Have a mini concert featuring "A Minor Ensemble," "Driving Rhythm," and "Flamenco Mood (duet)." It would be ideal to have the class form duets to play for extra credit for the class. It is fun to have them create a group name. The duos will come to the front of the class, take an acknowledgement bow, sit down, announce the song title, and perform, finally standing up and taking a bow at the end. Show the students how to take a bow together by having one person in each group be the leader.

INNOVATIONS @HOME

Ask the class to research the history of music notation and tablature on the Internet. A brief paper or PowerPoint presentation can be assigned asking students to research and report on interesting notation and tablature developments.

SOUND EXPECTATIONS

The information in all of the lesson plans will help the instructor meet a wide variety of the National Standards for Music Education. Think of ways in which the following standards were integrated into your guitar classroom.

1. Singing, alone and with others, a varied repertoire of music.

2. Performing on instruments, alone and with others, a varied repertoire of music.

3. Improvising melodies, variations, and accompaniments.

4. Composing and arranging music within specified guidelines.

5. Reading and notating music.

6. Listening to, analyzing, and describing music.

7. Evaluating music and music performances.

8. Understanding relationships between music, the other arts, and disciplines outside the arts.

9. Understanding music in relation to history and culture.

Visit the NAfME website at http://www.menc.org/ for more guidance in working with the standards as they are known to music teachers.

LESSON 3 | Accidentals, the E Minor Chord

GOALS
- Students will learn the function of sharp (♯), flat (♭), and natural (♮) signs and understand their relationship to the guitar fingerboard—a sharp raises a note by one fret, a flat lowers a note by one fret.
- Students will play the E minor chord and compare it to the E major chord.
- Reinforce eighth notes with familiar rock and blues bass line-type patterns.

NATIONAL STANDARDS
NS2 (Playing), NS5 (Reading), NS6 (Listening), NS9 (History & Culture)

LESSON 3A (Accidentals, Page 8)

1. DVD chapter 8 explains and demonstrates accidentals on the guitar.

   a. Demonstrate and explain the function of sharp, flat, and natural signs.

   b. With hands in the 1st position, ask students to play as you randomly call out natural notes (E, F, G, A, B, C) and then sharp or flat notes.

   c. Worksheet #6 is available as a free, reproducible document at www.alfred.com/SoundInnovations/ SIGuitar. It is a fill-in style worksheet designed to reinforce accidentals and note position on the fingerboard.

2. Line 16: "Strength Builder." This chromatic exercise is an excellent warm-up and can be used to start off any lesson or practice session. Important: when playing this exercise, once a finger presses on a note/fret it should remain there as the pattern ascends and only be released when necessary as the notes descend.

3. Line 17: "Crime Theme No. 1." This is loosely based on the classic guitar and bass line figure "Peter Gunn." Listen to CD track 17. Ask the class to play along. All students should perform both the guitar parts. Demonstrate the **brush stroke** used in Guitar 2.

OBSERVATIONAL ASSESSMENTS

- Left hand: Fingers curved, playing on fingertips. Fingers do not interfere with adjacent strings. Thumb centered behind neck. Students are using the correct fingers: in 1st position that is 1st finger/1st fret, 2nd finger/2nd fret, and so on. This will change when we move to 2nd position.

- Right hand: Pick is held between thumb and index finger, hand is relaxed, and all notes are played with a down-stroke of the pick, in which the pick strikes the string with a downward attack, coming to rest on the 5th string.

- Rhythm: Notes should be played with a steady eighth-note pulse. In "Crime Theme No. 1," Guitars 1 and 2 should be able to hold a steady rhythm and perform together.

LESSON 3B (the E Minor Chord, Page 9)

1. DVD chapter 9 introduces the E minor chord.

   a. Ask students to look at the E and Em chord grids at the top of page 9 of the student book. Ask them to describe the difference.

   b. Students should play the E major chord, and then by simply removing the 1st finger from the 3rd string they can play the E minor chord. Ask them to listen to and describe the difference between the sound of each chord.

   Note *Make sure that, when they play the Em chord, the 3rd string is ringing clearly. If it is accidentally muted, the minor 3rd of the chord (the open G string) will not make a sound, so although it might look like Em, it will not sound as a minor chord.*

   c. Ask the students to listen to the G♯ moving down to G when they play E–Em. Then ask them to sing the G♯ to G note change as they play the two chords. Sing with them to help.

2. Line 19: "Crime Theme No. 2." Students should listen to MP3 track 19 and/or DVD chapter 10 before they practice and perform line 19. Point out that this example will be performed in 2nd position, in which the 1st finger is at the 2nd fret—see DVD chapter 10 for a full explanation. This example is based on the opening guitar/bass riff to the James Bond theme. Guitar 1 plays the bass line figure and Guitar 2 plays an Em chord.

3. Line 20: "Blues Bass." Students should listen to MP3 track 20 before attempting to play this example. The Guitar 1 part is a classic rock and blues bass riff that they will likely play the rest of their lives, in many forms and variations. Circulate throughout the class checking hand position and fingering and assisting with any difficulties. This example is also in 2nd position.

   Note *Why 2nd position? Lines 19 and 20 could be played in the 1st position, but the fingering would be much weaker and much more difficult (because these figures are based around the 2nd and 4th frets). Any experienced guitarist would choose 2nd position for these. Our approach is to play "guitaristically" at all times.*

OBSERVATIONAL ASSESSMENTS

- When playing the E minor chord, fingers should be curved and not interfering with, or muting, adjacent strings. Be especially aware of the 3rd string. It should clearly ring out. That is the note that makes the chord minor. Ask students to hold the Em chord and play one string at a time. All six strings should ring clearly.

- Are students playing with a steady tempo?

- Clarify any misunderstandings related to accidentals. This is important to their continued understanding of the logic of the guitar fingerboard.

SOUND ADVICE

To reinforce music literacy, accidentals, and fingerboard understanding, print and distribute Worksheet #6 from www.alfred.com/SoundInnovations/SIGuitar.

INNOVATIONS @HOME

Ask the class to research the music to the Peter Gunn and James Bond themes. Listen to various versions of each song.

SOUND EXPECTATIONS

- Use line 16 to reinforce the concept of accidentals. However, students will likely start playing the pattern from memory very quickly, which is okay since we will be using this pattern as a stretching exercise throughout the book.

- Students should be able to play E to E minor with all six strings ringing clearly.

- Line 19: "Crime Theme No. 2." Students should place their left hand 1st finger firmly at the 2nd fret B note and keep it there throughout the entire bass line. It will serve as a base to anchor the hand properly in position.

- Line 20: "Blues Bass." Again, if students anchor their left hand 1st finger firmly at the 2nd fret B note and keep it there throughout the entire bass line, it will serve as a base to anchor the hand properly in position and make note-mistakes much less likely.

- In general, within about a week of practice time, most students will be able to play the example on these two pages with reasonable accuracy.

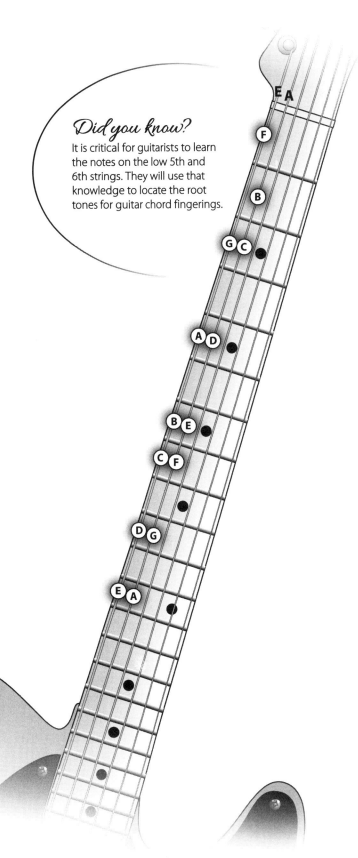

Did you know?
It is critical for guitarists to learn the notes on the low 5th and 6th strings. They will use that knowledge to locate the root tones for guitar chord fingerings.

9

LESSON 4 | $\frac{3}{4}$ Time Signature and Fingerpicking

GOALS
- Learn the $\frac{3}{4}$ time signature and dotted half notes.
- Learn the terms "block chord" and "arpeggio."
- Play simple bass/melody line examples with correct rhythm.
- Strum chords: E, F Flamenco, and G Flamenco.
- Explore fingerpicking technique.

NATIONAL STANDARDS NS2 (Playing), NS5 (Reading), NS6 (Listening), NS8 (Making Connections)

LESSON 4A ($\frac{3}{4}$ Time Signature and Malaguena Melody, Page 10)

1. Sound Check: Check tuning with the CD tuning track or an electronic tuner. It is a good idea to do the stretching exercises at the beginning of the class. Check the students' left-hand nails—it is important that they keep them short. Longer nails on the left hand make it extremely difficult to execute chords and melodies. It is fine to have longer nails on the right hand.

2. DVD chapter 11 introduces and demonstrates the $\frac{3}{4}$ time signature and conducting pattern (also see Appendix 7, specifically the bottom of page 55 of the student book).

3. Demonstrate and describe the dotted half note. Also point out the rhythm slash notation for a dotted half rhythm at the top of the page and how it relates to Guitar 2 in "Malaguena Melody." You can help the student feel the rhythm by conducting the $\frac{3}{4}$ pattern and having them strum an E chord for four measures. Make sure the class is in sync with the downbeats and the chords are held for a full measure. Add the F Flamenco chord to the mix, and finally the G Flamenco chord. Call out a rotation of these chords for the students to perform.

   Note *When setting up the guitar classroom make sure you have enough room between each student's chair to circulate throughout the class to check hand position and assist with any difficulties.*

4. DVD chapter 12 and CD track 21 both demonstrate "Malaguena Melody." Have the students pay attention to the musical "road map" by following repeat signs and directions such as "Repeat 2 times." Ask students to be aware of the volume balance between Guitar 1 and Guitar 2. Review bass ledger lines with the class. Additionally, you can have the students say the names of the pitches for the melody in "Malaguena Melody."

5. Divide the class in half, ask one group to play Guitar 1 and the other Guitar 2, then switch parts. All students should learn all guitar parts for each song in the book. Keep in mind that students can use the DVD track as a review resource and can play along with either the DVD or the CD.

6. Guitar 1 should use 2nd position fingerings for measures 1 and 2 and return to 1st position for the rest. Review 2nd position from page 9 of the student book.

OBSERVATIONAL ASSESSMENTS

- Left hand: Fingers curved, fingertips are perpendicular to the fretboard so fingers do not interfere with adjacent strings. Thumb is centered behind neck.
- Right hand: Pick is held between thumb and index finger, hand is relaxed, and all notes are played with a down-stroke of the pick.
- Rhythm: Notes should be played with a steady beat. All musical "road maps" are followed. Ensemble performances are balanced.

LESSON 4B (Fingerpicking, Pages 10–11)

1. DVD chapter 13 introduces fingerpicking technique as does CD track 22. View DVD chapter 13 carefully and discuss any questions before moving on. It is very important to spend time on the basics of fingerstyle performance so that the students are not practicing poor right-hand technique. The bottom of page 10 in the student book is an explanation of fingerpicking basics. Students should revisit the DVD often to observe and understand right-hand technique. Also, there is a Right-Hand Technique Builder handout available online that you can print and distribute to the class.

2. Present the overview of fingerpicking from the bottom of page 10 to the class. Students should understand the right-hand classifications: *p* (thumb), *i* (index), *m* (middle), *a* (ring). Demonstrate to the class that fingers arch towards the palm moving from the knuckle joint at the base of each finger. When finger *a* is used, the right-hand pinky will move in tandem with it.

3. Line 22: "Thumb and Fingers." Demonstrate how to play the Em chord. Students will hold the chord and plant the right hand thumb and fingers on the 6th, 3rd, 2nd, and 1st strings. Circulate throughout the class checking right hand position and assisting with any difficulties.

   a. Students will play the example as written, with a steady quarter-note rhythm. The proper right-hand motion can be described as being like catching a fly with your right hand. After playing the chord, re-plant the fingers on the strings in preparation of the next attack.

   b. Students should observe the right hand—fingers are relaxed and naturally arched and move from the knuckle joint. Listen to MP3 track 13 then ask students to perform line 22.

c. Use the SI Player to start at a very slow tempo so that the students can execute the exercise. Define the terms "block chord" and "arpeggio" and ask the class whether they are playing a series of block chords or arpeggios.

4. Line 23: "Thumb Then Fingers." In this example, the thumb plays beats 1 and 3 and the fingers pluck on beats 2 and 4. This creates a full-sounding accompaniment pattern, as if the thumb is functioning as a bass player and the fingers are the guitar player. Tell the students to keep in mind that the thumb should be in front of the fingers and fires independent of the fingers (see DVD).

a. Demonstrate how fingers *i*, *m*, and *a* arch towards the palm, flexing from the finger joint at the base of each finger.

b. Use the SI Player to start at a very slow tempo so that the students can execute the exercise. When moving to the eighth notes in bars 3 and 4 ask the class to count out loud and tap their feet so the tap is on the beat and the "and" of each beat is at the apex of raising the foot.

5. Line 24: "Thumb and Fingers Separated." The goal of this example is to help students begin to control one finger at a time. Students will plant their fingers in position before starting:

a. First, the thumb plays measure 1. All three fingers should remain planted on the top three strings while the thumb plays. The thumb should return to rest on the 6th string at the end of measure 1 and can stay there, serving as a base as the fingers play the remaining three measures.

b. Next, the index finger plays. At the end of measure 2, the index finger should remain relaxed and not return to rest on the 3rd string.

c. Next, the middle finger plays the 2nd string. When measure 3 is complete the middle and index fingers should remain relaxed and should not replant on their respective strings yet.

d. Finally, the index finger (*a*) plays. When measure 4 is complete, all three fingers should now re-plant on their respective strings to begin the exercises again.

6. Line 25: "Fingerpicking Pattern No. 1."

a. Review how to conduct the $\frac{4}{4}$ pattern.

b. Play MP3 track 25 and have the class conduct with the recording. Make the class aware of the exercise's "road map" noting that it will be played twice.

c. Use the SI Player to set a slow tempo that the students can play along with. Students should play this pattern until it flows easily from memory. It is critical that basic patterns like this one can be performed from memory so that they can easily be applied to any chord.

OBSERVATIONAL ASSESSMENTS

• All fingerpicking patterns should be in time with a solid beat.

• As students gain confidence at slower tempos, gradually keep raising the tempo in small increments via a metronome, drum machine, or the SI Player. The recorded tempos are the goal.

• The right hand is relaxed with fingers planted before starting to play. Students are using the tips of their fingers. Fingers move from the knuckle where the finger joins the hand. When *a* is fired, the pinky moves sympathetically with it; it is not left behind or anchored on the guitar body. Fingers are independent and do not interfere with each other.

SOUND ADVICE

"Sometimes you want to give up the guitar. But if you stick with it, you're gonna be rewarded."

— JIMI HENDRIX

• Expand on the lesson by asking students to apply "Fingerpicking Pattern No. 1" to the following two chord progressions (chord sequences):

  1. E–Em–E–Em

  2. Am–Em–Am–Em (thumb plays the 5th string on the Am chord)

• Ask the class to describe the sound they associate with minor chords such as Em (sad, pretty, etc.)

• Always keep an eye on the students' fingerstyle technique. This skill does not happen overnight—it will take time, but the rewards are well worth the effort.

INNOVATIONS @HOME

Ask the class to research pick and finger styles of playing the guitar on the Internet using the following search terms: plectrum, flat pick, fingerstyle, fingerpicking, and Travis picking. A brief paper or PowerPoint presentation can be assigned asking students to research and report on the similarities and differences between each of these techniques.

SOUND EXPECTATIONS

Fingerpicking is a skill that comes with time and practice. The students will have numerous opportunities throughout the book to develop. At this point they may not be able to keep a smooth or continuous rhythm.

SOUND SUGGESTIONS

Develop a filing system for student work. If a hanging file carton is placed by the class entrance/exit with student names clearly marked the students can help you by placing his or her completed worksheets or projects into the file.

LESSON 5 | Fingerpicking in A Minor, Moving Chord Shapes, Acoustic Fantasy

GOALS
- Students will apply "Fingerpicking Pattern No. 1" (*p–i–m–a–p–i–m–a*).
- Students will use the basic Am chord shape to create new and interesting chords.
- Students will perform "Acoustic Fantasy" as an ensemble piece.

NATIONAL STANDARDS NS2 (Playing), NS3 (Improvising), NS4 (Composing), NS5 (Reading), NS6 (Listening)

LESSON 5A (Fingerpicking in A Minor, Page 12)

1. Play MP3 track 26 for the class.

  a. Students should prepare the right hand by placing thumb and fingers on the strings before they play.

  b. The left hand will shift between Am and E. **Both** chords share the exact same shape and fingering. To change from Am to E and back again quickly, lift all fingers off the strings, retain the chord shape, and transfer it over one string-set.

  c. Expansion Jam: If you have any advanced students that can improvise rock and blues solos, this is a perfect song to open up for a jam. Solos can be improvised using any of the following scales:

    i. A minor pentatonic

    ii. A blues

    iii. A minor

    iv. Advanced: A minor over the Am chords and A harmonic minor over the E chords (or just add the G# note to the A minor scale when playing over the E chord).

OBSERVATIONAL ASSESSMENTS

- Left hand: Fingers curved, playing on fingertips. Fingers do not interfere with adjacent strings. Thumb centered behind neck.

- Right hand: The thumb should sweep through the string, out from the guitar, towards the fingers. The fingers should remain curved and travel in an arc through the string towards the center of the palm. Thumb and fingers should remain relaxed and gently curved at all times; all motion should initiate from the first knuckle joint, not by bending the middle knuckle joint at the center of each finger.

- Students should change chords on the beat. This is an intermediate, long-term goal for absolute beginners.

LESSON 5B (Moving Chord Shapes and Acoustic Fantasy, Pages 12–13)

1. DVD chapter 14 demonstrates the concept and technique of moving the Am chord shape. MP3 track 27 does the same.

  a. In this lesson, students will take the Am chord shape and slide it to different positions on the neck, creating some very interesting and beautiful chords with just one simple chord fingering. The combination of open-string notes that don't change from chord to chord, and fretted notes that do change, creates very interesting sounds. This is a very useful concept that guitarists often use as a compositional device.

  b. First practice the three chords: Students should hold the Am chord, then slide the Am chord shape up to the 6th fret (one fret above the second fretboard marker). This creates a beautiful and complex-sounding chord that we have labeled Dm/A for now (actually Dm9). But the name of the chord is not important at this point. Only that it is a very interesting sound and pretty easy to play.

  c. Next slide the chord shape down from the 6th to the 3rd fret (first fretboard marker). This forms a type of Bm with an open A in the bass (actual name is Bm11).

TECHNIQUE TIPS

- Keep fingers locked on the Am chord shape as you slide up and down the strings. Don't allow the index finger to interfere with the ringing open 1st string.

- For accuracy in location of the correct frets, focus on the index finger: for the Am it is at the 1st fret, for the Dm chord move it up to the 6th fret, and for the Bm move it down to the 3rd fret.

- Practice strumming each chord, one bar each, and changing on the beat. Once students are comfortable with that, have them apply "Fingerpicking Pattern No. 1" to the chords to play the Guitar 2 part in "Acoustic Fantasy." Guitar 1 is the melody.

OBSERVATIONAL ASSESSMENTS

• Are students maintaining the chord shape as they slide their hands into position on the neck? Assist students with maintaining the shape and locating the correct position on the neck by focusing on the location of the left hand index finger.

• Are all strings ringing? The open high E string is critical to creating the interesting chord sounds that we are looking for.

SOUND ADVICE

Many, many songwriter/guitarists experiment with moving chord shapes as a compositional tool. Distribute Worksheet #7, found at www.alfred.com/SoundInnovations/SIGuitar. Ask students to experiment with moving the E and Am chord shapes around until they find a chord sequence that they really like. They can use these worksheets to indicate their chord sequence and then fill in the shape in the blank and indicate the fret position.

INNOVATIONS @HOME

Students should practice "Acoustic Fantasy" and work on the above composition assignment.

SOUND EXPECTATIONS

• Some students will have difficulty locating the correct frets. Again, focusing on the location of the left hand index finger will help tremendously. Also, students should memorize that all guitars have markers at the 3rd and 5th frets. That will help them move around the neck with confidence.

• The fingerpicking pattern can also be a challenge. Fingerpicking is a long-term goal. For now, they should just do their best. It is also possible to play the same pattern with a pick or to just strum the chords instead of playing the arpeggio-style pattern.

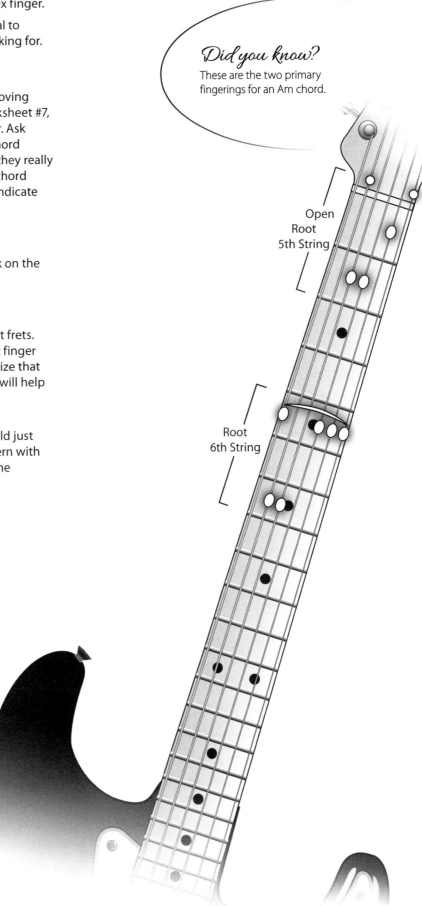

Did you know?
These are the two primary fingerings for an Am chord.

Open
Root
5th String

Root
6th String

13

LESSON 6 | Review and Assessment

 GOALS
- **Review key songs.**
- **Perform in groups.**
- **Solidify notes on the 5th and 6th strings, chords learned to date, fingerpicking, and strum patterns.**
- **Assess student progress and determine individual needs and goals for progress.**

 NATIONAL STANDARDS
NS2 (Playing), **NS3** (Improvising), **NS4** (Composing), **NS5** (Reading), **NS6** (Listening), **NS7** (Evaluating), **NS8** (Making Connections), **NS9** (History & Culture)

LESSON 6A: REVIEW AND OBSERVATIONAL ASSESSMENT (Pages 4–9)

1. Review and assess "Flamenco Mood (duet)" (page 5)

   a. Ask the class to break into small groups. A group leader should be picked for each. Each group will practice "Flamenco Mood (duet)." The group leader should conduct the practice session and also ask the group to switch parts once the ensemble begins to sound polished. Students should assist each other as is possible.

   b. Observe each group and for each student make note of the following:

      i. Left and right hand position—who looks good and who needs help?

      ii. Are students able to maintain a steady beat, keeping Guitars 1 and 2 together at all times? Who needs assistance with single-line melody work and who needs help with chords and strumming?

      iii. Is there a nice blend between guitar parts? Are there dynamics?

2. Review and assess "A Minor Ensemble" (page 7)

   a. Ask the class to break into small groups. A group leader should be picked for each. Each group will practice "A Minor Ensemble." The group leader should conduct the practice session and also ask the group to switch parts once the ensemble begins to sound polished. Students should assist each other as is possible.

   b. Observe each group and for each student make note of the following:

      i. Left and right hand position—who looks good and who needs help?

      ii. Are students able to maintain a steady beat, keeping Guitars 1 and 2 together at all times? Who needs assistance with single-line melody work and who needs help with chords and strumming?

      iii. Are students able to count and feel the quarter-note pulse (Guitar 2) and synchronize it with the eighth-note melody/bass line?

      iv. Is there a nice blend between guitar parts? Are there dynamics?

3. Review and assess lines 17, 19, and 20 (all blues bass line-type figures, pages 8–9)

   a. Ask class to break into small groups. A group leader should be picked for each. Each group will practice lines 17, 19, and 20. The group leader should conduct the practice session and also ask the group to switch parts once the ensemble begins to sound polished. Students should assist each other as is possible.

   b. Observe each group and for each student make note of the following:

      i. Left and right hand position—who looks good and who needs help?

      ii. Are students able to maintain a steady beat, keeping Guitars 1 and 2 together at all times? Who needs assistance with single-line melody work and who needs help with chords and strumming?

      iii. Are students able to count and feel the quarter-note pulse while playing steady eighth notes (Guitar 1) and chords (Guitar 2)?

      iv. Is there a nice blend between guitar parts? Are there dynamics?

LESSON 6B: REVIEW AND OBSERVATIONAL ASSESSMENT (Pages 10–13)

1. Review and assess line 21, "Malaguena Melody."

a. Each group will practice line 21. The group leader will conduct the practice session and also ask the group to switch parts once the ensemble begins to sound polished. Students should assist each other as is possible.

b. Observe each group and for each student make note of the following:

i. Left and right hand position—who looks good and who needs help?

ii. Are students able to maintain a steady beat, keeping Guitars 1 and 2 together at all times? Who needs assistance with single-line melody work and who needs help with chords and fingerpicking?

iii. Are students able to count and feel the quarter-note pulse while playing steady eighth notes (Guitar 1) and chords (Guitar 2)?

iv. Is there a nice blend between guitar parts? Are there dynamics? Guitar 2 may want to improvise brush strokes on some of the chord strums.

2. Review and assess line 28, "Acoustic Fantasy."

a. Each group will practice line 28. The group leader will conduct the practice session and also ask the group to switch parts once the ensemble begins to sound polished. Students should assist each other as is possible.

b. Observe each group and for each student make note of the following:

i. Left and right hand position—who looks good and who needs help?

ii. Are students able to maintain a steady beat, keeping Guitars 1 and 2 together at all times?

iii. Can students on Guitar 2 locate the correct fret position in time to play each succeeding chord?

iv. Who needs assistance with single-line melody work and who needs help with chords and fingerpicking?

v. Are students able to count and feel the quarter-note pulse while playing steady eighth notes (Guitar 1) and chords (Guitar 2)?

vi. Is there a nice blend between guitar parts? Are there dynamics?

LESSON 6C: FORMAL ASSESSMENTS FOR LEVEL 1

1. Students will form into groups/ensembles. Each ensemble will select one of the following pieces to perform for the class. There are significant differences in difficulty, however, the critical element is how musically the students perform their selected song.

a. "Flamenco Mood (Duet)" (page 5)

b. "A Minor Ensemble" (page 7)

c. "Malaguena Melody" (page 10)

d. "Acoustic Fantasy" (page 13)

2. Students should prepare their individual ensembles.

Call each ensemble to perform for the class. Use the downloadable Worksheet #8 to grade student performances. Or you can develop your own assessment sheet.

3. Download and hand out the peer assessment forms (Worksheet #9). Students should do peer assessments after each performance. Or you can create your own peer assessment forms with similar or the same criteria as above.

LESSON 1 | Notes on the 4th and 3rd Strings, New Chord: E7

GOALS
- **Learn to read and play D, E, F, G, and A.**
- **Review all notes.**
- **Play E7.**

NATIONAL STANDARDS NS2 (Playing), NS5 (Reading), NS6 (Listening), NS7 (Evaluating)

LESSON 1A
(Notes on the 4th and 3rd Strings, Page 14)

1. DVD chapter 16 introduces the new notes as does MP3 track 29.

2. Demonstrate and describe the D, E, F, G, and A notes. Call out the notes and have students play as requested. Students should play and say the notes together out loud. Circulate throughout the class checking hand position and fingering and assisting with any difficulties.

3. Worksheet #10 provides note reading reinforcement. It is available as a free, reproducible document at www.alfred.com/SoundInnovations/SIGuitar.

4. Line 30: "More Crime Theme No. 1." Perform line 30 with students and compare it to line 17 on page 8 of the student book. Ask students to describe the similarities.

OBSERVATIONAL ASSESSMENTS

- Left hand: Fingers curved, playing on fingertips. Fingers do not interfere with adjacent strings. Thumb centered behind neck.

- Right hand: Pick is held between thumb and index finger, hand is relaxed, and all notes are played with a down-stroke of the pick: pick strikes the string with a downward attack, towards the floor, coming to rest on the 5th string.

- Rhythm: Notes should be played with a steady beat. Students should use correct counting.

LESSON 1B (the E7 Chord, Page 14)

1. Line 31: Demonstrate and describe the E7 chord. Listen to MP3 track 31 with the class.

   a. Students should practice alternating between the E and E7 chords. Ask them to listen very carefully to the middle E of the E chord as it moves down to the open D. Be aware that if students allow their fingers to accidently mute the 4th string, the E7 will look like an E7, but will not sound like an E7.

   b. Ask students to alternate between the two chords while singing the pitch change from E to D. This will help them hear and understand the critical difference between these two chords. It might help if they only strum the bottom three or four strings so the note change is emphasized.

2. Line 32: Play MP3 track 32 for the class. Break them into two groups. Group 1 plays the Guitar 1 part and group 2 plays the Guitar 2 part. Then switch.

3. Constant review is critical; many of the songs in this book will be mastered over a period of months, not days or weeks. Break students into 2–4 person ensembles and ask them to review and perform a piece from the following list:

   Page 5: "Flamenco Mood (duet)"
   Page 7: "A Minor Ensemble"
   Page 9: "Crime Theme No. 2" and "Blues Bass"
   Page 10: "Malaguena Melody"
   Page 13: "Acoustic Fantasy"

OBSERVATIONAL ASSESSMENTS

- When playing the E7 chord, fingers should be curved and not interfering with, or muting, adjacent strings, especially the open D. Ask students to hold the E7 chord and play one string at a time. All six strings should ring clearly.

- All duets should be in time with a solid beat.

- As students gain confidence suggest they add variety and interest by playing louder and softer, explore slower and faster tempos, etc.

SOUND ADVICE

*"I don't practice scales and exercises.
I spend all my time playing real songs
that I really want to play."*

— AN OLD FRIEND WHEN ASKED,
"WHY DO YOU ALWAYS SOUND SO GOOD?"

- To reinforce music literacy and ledger lines, print and distribute Worksheet #10 from www.alfred.com/SoundInnovations/SIGuitar.

- Play, or have an advanced student play, the E and E7 chords and ask the class to identify, by ear, which is being played. Ask them to describe the difference in sound between the two chords.

- Observe all duet rehearsal. Some, like "Flamenco Mood (duet)" and "A Minor Ensemble," should start sounding very polished.

INNOVATIONS @HOME

Students should be practicing at least 15 minutes per evening at home.

SOUND EXPECTATIONS

Students should be showing greater accuracy when changing chords and many should be able to change chords on the beat at slow tempos. It is critical that chords are memorized. It is not possible to change chords at tempo if the mind has any question as to the correct fingering.

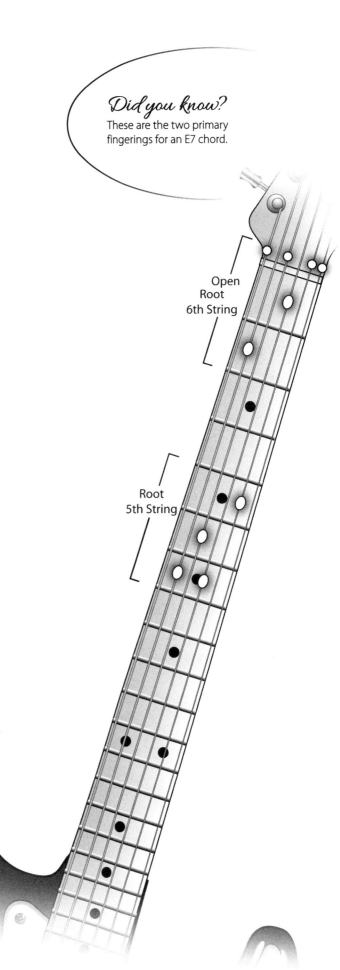

Did you know?
These are the two primary fingerings for an E7 chord.

Open
Root
6th String

Root
5th String

LESSON 2 | Chromatic Strength Builder with Chord Review

 GOALS
- Play the "Chromatic Strength Builder" exercise while saying each note out loud.
- Review all notes presented through page 15 of the student book.
- Play E and E7 and locate open string roots for future chords.

 NATIONAL STANDARDS NS2 (Playing), NS5 (Reading), NS6 (Listening), NS7 (Evaluating)

LESSON 2A
(the Chromatic Nature of the Guitar)

1. Discuss the concept of a **half step** and that it is the distance from one fret to the next. This distance is also called a **semitone**. Demonstrate the concept to the class by playing the 6th string F then the 2nd fret F♯. Have the students study the neck diagram at the top of page 15 of the student book. Review **accidentals** presented on page 8 with the class:

   A sharp (♯) placed in front of a note **raises** that note by a half step. For example, place a sharp in front of the note F and it becomes F♯ (F sharp), which is the fret between F and G.

   A flat (♭) placed in front of a note **lowers** that note by a half step. For example, place a flat in front of the note G and it becomes G♭ (G flat), which is located on the fret between F and G.

   Notice that "F♯" and "G♭" are different names for the same note. In musical terms they are called **enharmonics**—notes that sound the same but have different names. Ask the students to locate notes that do not have enharmonics between them in the diagram at the top of page 15 (E–F and B–C).

   An important rule in music is that when you use a sharp or flat, it will remain in effect for the remainder of the bar (measure) or until a natural sign (♮) cancels the sharp or flat. The term "accidental" refers to sharps, flats, and naturals.

2. Explain the term **chromatic sequence**—a series or sequence of notes moving up or down in half steps (a "chromatic" line).

   a. Use **sharps** when the line is ascending

   b. Use **flats** when the line is descending

   This reduces the number of accidentals required. Demonstrate and describe the idea of a musical sequence and how it relates to "Chromatic Strength Builder."

3. Demonstrate how to draw an accidental, then hand out blank manuscript paper and have the students practice drawing sharp, flat, and natural signs. In addition, students can copy the music notation from "Chromatic Strength Builder." Ask if the notation follows the concept of ascending lines using sharps and descending lines using flats.

4. Call out the notes and have students play as requested. Students should play and say the notes together out loud. Circulate throughout the class checking hand position and fingering and assisting with any difficulties.

5. Play the MP3 track for "Chromatic Strength Builder." Use the SI Player to slow the line to a tempo at which the students can play with minimal mistakes.

OBSERVATIONAL ASSESSMENTS

- Students should hold the fingers down when playing the ascending chromatic line, and slightly lift the fingers when playing the descending chromatic line.
- Students should notice that each line uses the same fingering but on a different string set.
- Left hand: fingers curved, playing on fingertips. Fingers do not interfere with adjacent strings. Thumb centered behind neck.
- Right hand: Pick is held between thumb and index finger, hand is relaxed, and all notes are played with a down-stroke of the pick: pick strikes the string with a downward attack, towards the floor, coming to rest on following string.
- Rhythm: Notes should be played with a steady beat. Students are using correct counting.

LESSON 2B
(the E Family Chord Review, Pages 9 and 14)

1. Hand out the Supplemental Chord Chart (available online) and let the students keep this as an aid. Demonstrate and describe the E, E7, and Em chords.

2. Students should practice alternating between E, E7, and Em. Ask them to listen very carefully to the notes of the E chords as they change. Be aware that if the students allow their fingers to accidentally mute the 4th string on E7 or the 3rd string on Em, the chords will look correct but will not sound as E7 and Em.

3. Ask students to alternate between E and E7 while singing the pitch change from E to D. Also have them alternate between the E and Em chords while singing the pitch change from G♯ to G. This will help them hear and understand the critical difference between these chords. It might help if they only strum the bottom three or four strings so the note change is emphasized.

4. Also ask the students to practice alternating from E or E7 to Am, and from Am to Em.

OBSERVATIONAL ASSESSMENTS

• When playing the above chords, fingers should be curved and not interfering with, or muting, adjacent strings—especially the open D and G strings. Ask students to hold the E, E7, Em, and Am chords and play one string at a time for each. All strings should always ring clearly.

• As students gain confidence suggest they add variety and interest by playing louder and softer, explore slower and faster tempos, etc.

SOUND ADVICE

"Listening is the key to everything good in music."
— PAT METHENY

• Have the students review the warm-ups on DVD track 44 and illustrated on page 52 of the student book.

• Inform the students that "Chromatic Strength Builder" and its possible variations are great warm-ups to play right after stretching and flexing the hands.

• Play, or have an advanced student play, the E, Em, and E7 chords and ask the class to identify, by ear, which is being played.

• Ask them to describe the difference in sound between the major, minor, and seventh chords.

INNOVATIONS @HOME

• Students should find time for practicing at least 15 minutes per day at home. This time should be consistent for each day, such as before school or after school in the evening. The more time they spend on an instrument, the more familiar all aspects of it will become.

• Hand out blank chord frames (available online) and ask the students to draw in the E, E7, Em, and Am as they are presented in the Supplemental Chord Chart. Have them fill in a complete line of E chords including fingerings and open strings and then strum the chord. Underneath this line they should fill in the E7 chord with appropriate fingerings and then strum that chord, following up with Em and finally Am.

SOUND EXPECTATIONS

• Students should be showing greater accuracy when playing the chromatic lines and understand how accidentals work.

• Students should be able to change chords on the beat, at medium tempos. It is critical that chords are memorized and can be visualized. It is not possible to change chords, at tempo, unless the students have memorized and can visualize each chord.

LESSON 3 | The Blues Song Form and the Blues Boogie Rhythm

 GOALS
- Discuss and analyze the 12-bar blues song form.
- Identify the I, IV, and V chords from a scale.
- Learn A5–A6, D5–D6, and E5–E6.
- Learn the classic blues boogie rhythm pattern.
- Apply the palm mute technique.

NATIONAL STANDARDS NS2 (Playing), NS5 (Reading), NS6 (Listening), NS7 (Evaluating), NS8 (Making Connections)

ABOUT THE BLUES

Blues music developed in the early 1900s from a variety of origins such as early spirituals, field hollers (sung by workers in the cotton fields), and the gospel music performed in rural Southern black churches. Blues was the music that was performed at parties, dances, and the roadhouse. Often the blues was performed in secret, since the local churches usually forbade their members from performing secular, or nonreligious, music.

Modern blues has been shaped by many sources and regions, but the two primary influences are:

- Acoustic music of the 1920s and '30s, mostly from rural Southern regions such as the Mississippi Delta and North Carolina. Early rural blues artists include Robert Johnson, Rev. Gary Davis, and Charlie Patton. Typically this kind of blues is performed by a solo guitarist/singer on an acoustic guitar, fingerstyle.

- The more sophisticated electric urban blues of the 1940s. Early electric blues artists include Muddy Waters, Howlin' Wolf, T-Bone Walker, and B.B. King, who came along a little later. This style of blues centered around Chicago and was usually performed on electric guitars with a full band.

- Blues has evolved since its early beginnings and has influenced many modern styles of music, especially jazz and rock.

LESSON 3A (Blues Song Form, Page 16)

1. DVD chapter 17 introduces the blues song form. MP3 track 34 also contains a full explanation of the blues form.

2. Play the blues demo from the end of MP3 track 34 for the class. Next play tracks 18, 26, and 35. Each of these is a 12-bar blues. Help the class to identify the I, IV, and V chords by ear. Note that tracks 18 and 26 both move to the IV chord in bar 10—this change is the single most common blues variation.

3. Distribute Worksheet #11 to the class. On it they will fill in the I, IV, and V chords into 12-bar blues song forms in three different keys.

4. Play MP3 track 36 for the class. The guitar part that they will hear is called a "boogie pattern." This is a fundamental pattern played throughout blues, rock, and country.

5. Now play MP3 track 35. It describes and demonstrates the chords the students will need to play the boogie pattern.

6. Count off a medium tempo and ask the class to repeatedly play line 35. Pay attention to the 2nd position fingerings for each of these chords. Circulate through the class assisting as needed. If you have any advanced guitarists in the class you can ask them to assist others.

OBSERVATIONAL ASSESSMENTS

- Are students able to identify the change from one chord to the next in a 12-bar blues?

- Are students able to label the changes as I, IV, and V?

- When playing the 5–6 power chord pattern, students should strike only two strings for each chord.

LESSON 3B (the Blues Boogie Rhythm, Page 17)

1. The class should watch DVD chapter 18. Remember, students should always view the DVD chapters before learning new material and then use them as a review resource.

   a. Begin by practicing the pattern for the A chord, then the D chord, and finally the E chord. Tip: Use the SI Player to slow track 36 down. Students can play along at a very slow tempo and gradually speed it up.

   b. When playing the power chords, fingers should be curved and not interfering with, or muting, the adjacent strings. Ask students to play the two notes of each power chord separately, making sure the notes ring clearly, then have them play through both notes for the two-note chord.

   c. Introduce palm muting (review the demonstration in DVD chapter 17). Ask the students to play "The Blues Boogie Rhythm" using the palm mute. Circulate throughout the class to assess that students can use the palm mute technique effectively.

   Note *Palm muting is valuable but optional at this time—don't go there if it causes problems or confusion.*

2. All power chords should be in time with a solid beat.

3. As students gain confidence, suggest they add variety and interest by playing louder and softer, explore slower and faster tempos, etc.

OBSERVATIONAL ASSESSMENTS

• Students should be playing with all down-strokes.

• When using the palm mute, strings should be muted and percussive, but the sound of the pitches should still be clear.

• Students have their fret hand 1st finger fixed firmly at the 2nd fret for each chord.

• Tempo should be rock steady.

SOUND ADVICE

"If you don't know the blues ... there's no point in picking up the guitar and playing rock 'n' roll or any other form of popular music."

— KEITH RICHARDS

• Distribute Worksheet #11 to the class. On it they will fill in the I, IV, and V chords into 12-bar blues song forms in three different keys.

• Bring in recordings of 12-bar blues songs to play for the class. Some classics would be:

"Johnny B. Goode" (Chuck Berry)
"Pride and Joy" (Stevie Ray Vaughan)
"Why I Sing the Blues" (B.B. King)
"Got My Mojo Working" (Muddy Waters)
"Killing Floor" (Howlin' Wolf)

• As the students do more research and worksheets and absorb supplemental materials, it may be a good idea to have them build a portfolio. Determine the type of binder or notebook to be used to organize the material. Pocket folders or three-ring notebooks are good suggestions. Make sure:

1. Each student has clearly labeled his or her notebook or binder

2. The students know they are responsible for keeping and organizing all of their guitar portfolio entries

3. Students can also include tape or CD recordings of their performances

Inform the students you will periodically review these for completeness and instruct them when to bring them to class.

INNOVATIONS @HOME

Ask students to find a recording of a 12-bar blues song.

SOUND EXPECTATIONS

Most students will be able to play the basic boogie pattern and change chords with reasonable accuracy.

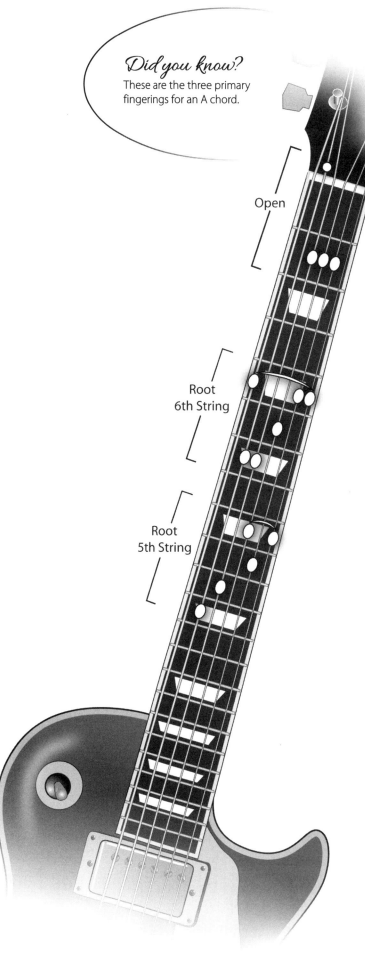

Did you know?
These are the three primary fingerings for an A chord.

Open

Root
6th String

Root
5th String

LESSON 4 | Fingerpicking in $\frac{3}{4}$

GOALS
- Discuss the elements and terms involved in $\frac{3}{4}$ fingerpicking patterns.
- Learn *pima*, in which *p* = thumb, *i* = index, *m* = middle, and *a* = ring finger. Also, planting the fingers and following through.
- Perform and practice $\frac{3}{4}$ fingerpicking patterns. First with a quarter note pattern and then with an eighth note pattern.
- Perform and practice a $\frac{3}{4}$ fingerpicking pattern with the Am and E chord forms.

NATIONAL STANDARDS NS2 (Playing), NS5 (Reading), NS6 (Listening), NS7 (Evaluating), NS8 (Making Connections)

FINER POINTS OF TECHNIQUE

Fingerpicking is an exciting aspect of guitar playing. Please tell students that it is acceptable to take time to understand and successfully execute this technique. By using tablature with rhythm stems, the process involved in studying and performing fingerstyle patterns is simplified. It is important to realize that once these patterns are set in motion they will generally continue to repeat throughout the song.

LESSON 4A (Fingerpicking in $\frac{3}{4}$, Page 18)

1. DVD chapter 19 introduces fingerpicking in $\frac{3}{4}$. MP3 track 37 also contains a full explanation of the basic fingerpicking pattern in $\frac{3}{4}$ (thumb–pluck–pluck).

2. Play MP3 track 37 for the class.

   a. Count off at a slow tempo and ask the class to repeatedly play line 37. Students should plant the thumb and fingers on the strings before playing at the beginning of the exercise.

   > **Note** *Many teachers advocate planting the fingers at the beginning of each measure, however, once the correct tempo is achieved, that approach results in a choppy and unnatural sound. Have students plant their fingers before beginning to play, but it's not necessary to replant the fingers in the middle of performing.*

   b. Fingers move in a gentle arc from the knuckle where they meet the hand. Circulate throughout the class assisting as needed. Note that fingering all the notes of the Em chord, even though they are not all played during the exercise, is a good habit to develop—if a wrong string is accidentally struck, the notes will still sound good.

OBSERVATIONAL ASSESSMENTS

- Are students able to isolate the thumb–pluck–pluck articulations cleanly?

- Are students able to place the fingers on the appropriate strings—*i* on the 3rd string, *m* on the 2nd string, and *a* on the 1st string—at the proper time and maintain a steady rhythm?

- Are the students moving their fingers in an arc from the knuckle where the fingers meet the hand, or are they clutching or snapping the strings?

- Keep in mind that when strings 3–2–1 are plucked by *i–m–a*, the pinky will move sympathetically with the other fingers.

- When the students are playing the exercise, hold your hand close to their plucking hand. If they are executing the study properly, the top of their hand will not touch yours.

LESSON 4B (Fingerpicking Pattern No. 2, Page 18)

1. The class should watch DVD chapter 19 for line 38. Remember that students need to view the DVD chapters before learning new material and can also use them as a review resource.

   a. Begin by planting the fingers on the strings for the Em chord as required for "Fingerpicking Pattern No. 2." Tip: Use the SI Player to slow track 38 down. Students can play along at a very slow tempo and gradually speed it up.

   b. When playing this pattern, the right hand needs to be relaxed with the wrist slightly arched and the hand slightly tilted towards the neck. This will help the right hand fingertips line up with the strings. Ask students to play the example slowly, making sure all notes are played clearly and in time.

2. The pattern needs to be played with a very steady beat. The thumb is the timekeeper, sounding on beats 1 and 3. When fingerpicking we often think of the thumb as the bass player and the fingers as the guitar player. This pattern is a good example of that.

3. As students gain confidence ask them to apply the same fingerpicking pattern to the E and E7 chords.

OBSERVATIONAL ASSESSMENTS

- Students should be playing with solid right hand technique.

- The sound of the notes should be clear.

- Execution should be steady when played at a slow tempo, and maintained as the tempo is slightly increased.

LESSON 4C (Fingerpicking in A Minor $\frac{3}{4}$, Page 18)

1. The class should watch DVD chapter 19 for example 39. Remember, students should view the DVD chapters before learning new material and then use them as a review resource.

   a. Begin by applying the $\frac{3}{4}$ fingerpicking pattern to the Am chord and then the E chord. Then ask the class to perform line 39. It may help the students if they can play along with track 39 at a very slow tempo and gradually speed it up, so remember that you can use the SI Player to slow the music down.

   b. Use the thumb to strum the final Am chord.

2. As students gain confidence suggest they add variety and interest by playing louder and softer, explore slower and faster tempos, etc.

OBSERVATIONAL ASSESSMENTS

• Students should be playing the pattern for both chords with solid right hand technique.

• The sound of the notes should be clear.

• Students should use the appropriate left-hand fingering for each chord.

• Execution should be steady.

SOUND ADVICE

"My guitar is not a thing. It is an extension of myself. It is who I am."

— JOAN JETT

• Review Worksheet #12 with the class. In it they will be guided through creating their own eight-measure chord progression.

• Circulate throughout the class and scan for students who need help with right hand technique. They should spend extra time watching the DVD and emulating what they see.

INNOVATIONS @HOME

Ask students to explore YouTube to find videos they can share with the class of great guitarists fingerpicking.

SOUND EXPECTATIONS

• Most students will be able to play the three basic $\frac{3}{4}$ fingerstyle patterns and change chords with reasonable accuracy while maintaining consistent *pima* alternations.

• The following songs can be used as supplemental materials for performance, playing by ear, singing, and jamming.

Songs that can be played with one chord
The Beat Goes On (Sonny & Cher)
Coconut (Harry Nilsson)
Chain of Fools (Aretha Franklin)
Electric Avenue (Eddy Grant)
I'm a Man (Bo Diddley)
It's Raining, It's Pouring
Loser (Beck)
On the Road Again (Canned Heat)
This Old Man

Songs that can be played with two chords
The Banana Boat Song (Day-O)
Born in the U.S.A. (Bruce Springsteen)
Down by the Riverside
Dreams (Fleetwood Mac)
Drunken Sailor
Eleanor Rigby (The Beatles)
Feelin' Alright (Traffic)
Give Peace a Chance (John Lennon)
A Horse with No Name (America)
Jambalaya (Hank Williams)
Oh My Darling, Clementine
Paperback Writer (The Beatles)
Row, Row, Row, Your Boat
Run Through the Jungle (Creedence Clearwater Revival)
Streets of Laredo
Tom Dooley
Tulsa Time (Don Williams)

Songs that can be played with three chords
The Lion Sleeps Tonight (made famous by The Tokens)
Happy Birthday
John Brown's Body
My Eyes Have Seen the Glory
Silent Night
Margaritaville (Jimmy Buffett)
Moondance (Van Morrison)
Twist and Shout (made famous by both The Isley Brothers, The Beatles, and others)
Bad Moon Rising (Creedence Clearwater Revival)
Blowin' in the Wind (Bob Dylan)
All Right Now (Free)
Brown Eyed Girl (Van Morrison)
Amazing Grace
Get Back (The Beatles)
Guantanamera
Hava Nagila
He's Got the Whole World in His Hands
Hound Dog (made most famous by Elvis Presley)
Johnny B. Goode (Chuck Berry)
Michael, Row the Boat Ashore (Peter, Paul and Mary)
Rock Around the Clock (Bill Haley & His Comets)
Surfin' USA (The Beach Boys)
Sweet Home Alabama (Lynyrd Skynyrd)
The Tide Is High (The Paragons)

LESSON 5 | Plaisir d' Amour

GOALS

• **Learn three new chords: G, C, and D.**
• **Apply the $\frac{3}{4}$ fingerpicking pattern to the chords of "Plaisir d' Amour."**
• **Explore the key signature for G major.**
• **Learn quarter and whole note rests and ties.**

NATIONAL STANDARDS   **NS2** (Playing), **NS3** (Improvising), **NS4** (Composing), **NS5** (Reading), **NS6** (Listening)

LESSON 5A (New Chords G, C, and D, Page 19)

1. DVD chapter 20 is a full performance of this song. Students should watch and discuss before playing.

2. Begin by asking the students to strum the chords to "Plaisir d' Amour." They can strum quarter notes or dotted half notes—either way, the challenge is to memorize the chord fingerings and change chords on the beat.

3. While playing each chord, the student should look ahead and try to visualize the next chord's fingering so that he or she can change chords without dropping the beat. It will take several days or longer for most students to change chords without dropping beats. It is critical that the chord fingerings are memorized.

4. Create a simple chord study in $\frac{3}{4}$ using the $\frac{3}{4}$ fingerpicking pattern ("Fingerpicking Pattern No. 2") over G, C, and D.

   a. Ask the students to play the pattern over each chord, as shown below. Each slash equals a full bar of the chord:

   / G   /   /   /   /
   / C   /   /   /   /
   / D   /   / G   /   //

   b. For additional practice ask the class to play the same progression in $\frac{4}{4}$ using "Fingerpicking Pattern No. 1" on page 11 of the student book. Or, students can just strum the chords instead of fingerpicking.

OBSERVATIONAL ASSESSMENTS

• Assist students with fretting with their fingertips so that all strings ring clearly.

• Students should try to picture the shape and fingering of each chord before they play it. Specifically ask them to picture a chord, position their fingers, and play it.

LESSON 5B (Plaisir d' Amour, Page 19)

1. Play MP3 track 41. Students should always be familiar with a song before attempting to play it.

2. Divide the class in half and have one group play Guitar 1 and the other Guitar 2, then switch parts. All students should learn all guitar parts for each song in the book. Keep in mind that students can use the DVD chapter as a review resource and can play along with either the DVD or the CD.

3. Observe each group and for each student make note of the following.

   a. Left and right hand position, who looks good and who needs help?

   b. Guitar 1: Are they playing correct rhythms and holding the tied notes for the full value?

   c. Guitar 2: Students will be applying the $\frac{3}{4}$ fingerpicking pattern to each chord in the song. They should be able to play the pattern from memory so they can focus on playing the correct chord forms and strings. This pattern uses the thumb on beats 1 and 3. This may seem awkward at first, but students will soon find that the thumb is very strong, and using it this way helps keep time and establish a really strong rhythm.

4. Combine students into small ensembles so they can rehearse the songs with both parts. Circulate throughout the class, observe each group, and for each student make note of the following.

   a. Left and right hand position, who looks good and who needs help?

   b. Are students able to maintain a steady beat, keeping guitars 1 and 2 together at all times? Who needs assistance with single line melody work and who needs help with the fingerpicking pattern or the chord forms?

   c. Is there a nice blend between guitar parts? Are there dynamics?

   d. Optional: Instead of playing the fingerpicking pattern, some students on Guitar 2 can simply strum the chords with a steady quarter note rhythm.

OBSERVATIONAL ASSESSMENTS

- Students are counting and playing the melody with correct timing. Especially pay attention to the tied notes in bars 4 and 5.

- Chords are changing on the correct beat.

- Students are using a solid rhythm whether strumming or fingerpicking. Important: The accompaniment part provides the rhythmic foundation. It is not just a series of notes. Without strong rhythm it will not work.

SOUND ADVICE

"Shut Up 'N Play Yer Guitar."

— FRANK ZAPPA

INNOVATIONS @HOME

Ask students to take either the C chord or the D chord and create a song or chord pattern by moving those shapes around the neck until they find something they like.

SOUND EXPECTATIONS

- The G, C, and D chords are critical core guitar chord formations. Students make take several weeks or even longer before they can play them cleanly and in tempo. However, they will play these same chords in virtually every song they ever learn, so the reinforcement will happen naturally.

- Some students will take more naturally to fingerpicking than others. As long as they stick with it they will get the control and dexterity required. In the meantime any student having significant issues with fingerstyle can be encouraged to stick with strumming for now. There is nothing wrong with that—it is a very valid, useful, and common technique.

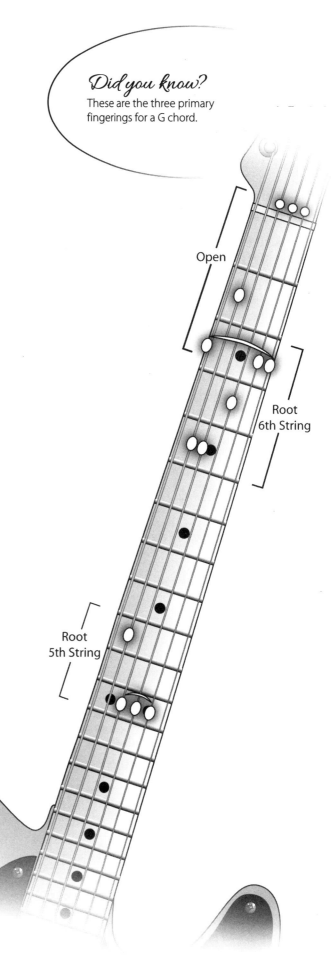

Did you know?
These are the three primary fingerings for a G chord.

Open

Root
6th String

Root
5th String

LESSON 6 | Review and Assessment

GOALS
- **Review key songs.**
- **Perform in groups.**
- **Solidify notes on the 3rd, 4th, 5th, and 6th strings; chords learned to date; fingerpicking; and strum patterns.**
- **Assess student progress and determine individual needs and goals for progress.**

NATIONAL STANDARDS **NS2** (Playing), **NS3** (Improvising), **NS4** (Composing), **NS5** (Reading), **NS6** (Listening), **NS7** (Evaluating), **NS8** (Making Connections)

LESSON 6A: REVIEW AND OBSERVATIONAL ASSESSMENT (Page 14)

1. Review and assess "More Crime Theme No. 1"

   a. Review the first and second endings.

   b. Play MP3 track 30 and have the students watch the score.

   c. Ask students to perform the music, then scan the class and for each student make note of the following:

      i. Left and right hand position and technique: who looks good and who needs help?

      ii. Are students able to maintain a steady beat? Who needs assistance with single line melody work and who needs help with chords and strumming?

      iii. Is the student using the pick to cleanly and smoothly switch between strings when required? Are there dynamics?

2. Review and assess "Note Review" (page 14)

   a. Ask the class to break into small groups. A group leader should be picked for each. Each group will practice "Note Review." The group leader will conduct the practice session and also ask the group to switch parts once the ensemble begins to sound polished. Students should assist each other when possible.

   b. Observe each group and for each student make note:

      i. Left and right hand position: who looks good and who needs help?

      ii. Are students able to maintain a steady beat, keeping guitars 1 and 2 together at all times? Who needs assistance with single line melody work and who needs help with chords and strumming?

      iii. Are students able to count and feel the quarter note pulse (Guitar 2) and synchronize it with the eighth note melody?

      iv. Is there a nice blend between guitar parts? Are there dynamics? Did they let the last chord ring for the full four beats?

   c. Point out to the class that this study can be used as a warm-up exercise.

3. Review and assess "Chromatic Strength Builder" (page 15)

   a. Ask the class to review and discuss the theory behind accidentals and how the concept of a half-step relates to the guitar.

   b. Observe the class as they perform and for each student make note:

      i. Left and right hand position: who looks good and who needs help?

      ii. Are students able to maintain a steady beat? Who needs assistance with single lines?

      iii. Are students able to count and feel the quarter note pulse while playing steady eighth notes?

      iv. Ask the students to start the study softly and gradually increase in volume. Are they able to handle dynamics?

LESSON 6B: REVIEW AND OBSERVATIONAL ASSESSMENT (Pages 16–17)

1. Review the section "Blues Song Form."

   a. Observe the class and for each student make note of their understanding of the materials presented in the text.

   b. Play MP3 track 34. Can students identify (by raising their hands) when a chord will be changed in the song form?

2. Review and assess line 36, "The Blues Boogie Rhythm."

   a. Observe the class and for each student make note of the following:

      i. Can students use the correct 2nd position sequence to play each succeeding power chord, all in time?

      ii. Who needs assistance with the pattern and who needs help with specific power chords?

      iii. Are students able to count and feel the quarter note pulse while playing steady eighth notes (Guitar 1) and chords (Guitar 2)

      iv. Is there a nice blend between guitar parts? Are there dynamics? Ask the students to mark in a specific measure to switch to palm muting.

LESSON 6C: REVIEW AND OBSERVATIONAL ASSESSMENT (Page 18)

1. Review and assess all three fingerpicking patterns on this page.

a. Observe the class and for each student make note of the following:

i. Can students use the correct right hand technique and play in time? Can they maintain the pattern when moving from the Am chord to the E chord?

ii. Who needs assistance with the pattern?

iii. Are students able to count and feel the quarter note pulse while playing steady eighths with the right hand?

iv. Can the student successfully substitute another chord, either Em or E7, for the E?

LESSON 6D: REVIEW AND OBSERVATIONAL ASSESSMENT (Page 19)

1. Review the new chords G, C, and D

a. Observe the class and for each student make note of the following:

i. Can the students visualize the new chords? Can they switch chords with the fingers moving as a unit, not one finger at a time?

ii. Can the students make the following chord changes smoothly? C–G, G–C, G–D, and D–G.

2. Review and assess line 41, "Plaisir d' Amour."

a. Observe the class and for each student make note of the following:

i. Can students correctly play the melody?

ii. Identify who needs assistance with the melody and who needs help with the fingerpicking pattern.

iii. Are students able to count and feel the quarter note pulse while playing steady eighth-note accompaniment with the fingerpicking part?

iv. Is there a nice blend between guitar parts? Are there dynamics? Ask the students to switch parts. How do they perform the new part?

LESSON 6E: FORMAL ASSESSMENTS FOR LEVEL 2

1. Students will form into groups/ensembles with one person on a part. Each ensemble will select one of the following pieces to perform for the class. The students will pick a name for their ensemble and announce it to the class before performing their selection. There are significant differences in difficulty, however, the critical element is how musically the students perform and present their selected song.

a. "Note Review" (page 14)

b. "The Blues Boogie Rhythm" (page 17)

c. "Plaisir d' Amour" (page 19)

2. Students will prepare their individual ensembles.

Call each ensemble to perform for the class. Use Worksheet #13 (www.alfred.com/SoundInnovations/SIGuitar) to grade student performances. Or, you can develop your own assessment sheet. Some points to consider in your ensemble assessments are below. In addition you can distribute Worksheet #13a for student/peer assessments.

a. Tuning

b. Musicality

c. Tone quality

d. Rhythm and tempo

e. Phrasing

f. Playing position

g. Expressiveness

LESSON 1 | Notes on the 2nd and 1st Strings

GOALS
- **Learn to read and play B, C, D, E, F, and G on the 2nd and 1st strings.**
- **Review.**

NATIONAL STANDARDS **NS1** (Singing), **NS2** (Playing), **NS5** (Reading), **NS6** (Listening), **NS8** (Making Connections), **NS9** (History & Culture)

LESSON 1A
(Notes on the 2nd and 1st Strings, Page 20)

1. Before introducing the new notes use line 33, "Chromatic Strength Builder," as a warm-up.

   a. Ask students to play line 33 from page 15 of the student book.

   b. Review the sharps and flats and discuss their location on the guitar neck (a sharp is up a fret and a flat is down a fret from the natural note).

   c. Students should be using all four left hand fingers—one finger per fret.

2. DVD chapter 21 introduces the new notes on page 20 of the student book, as does MP3 track 42.

   a. Demonstrate and describe the new notes. Call out the notes and have students play as requested. Students should play and say the notes together out loud. Circulate throughout the class checking hand position and fingering and assisting with any difficulties.

   b. Worksheet #14 provides note reading reinforcement. It is available as a free, reproducible document at www.alfred.com/SoundInnovations/SIGuitar.

3. Ask the class to play line 43. Students should play and say the notes aloud.

4. Listen to MP3 track 44 and then ask the class to play line 44. Circulate, assisting as needed.

5. Ask the class to apply the chromatic scale fingering from line 33 to the two new strings. Count a slow tempo and have them play and say the chromatic scale on the 2nd string then the 1st. Review the location of sharp and flat notes.

6. Ask the class to apply the chromatic scale to all six strings and have them say each note as they play.

OBSERVATIONAL ASSESSMENTS

- Left hand: Fingers curved, playing on fingertips. Fingers do not interfere with adjacent strings. Thumb centered behind neck. Students are using one finger per fret (1–2–3–4).

- Right hand: Pick is held between thumb and index finger, hand is relaxed, and all notes are played with a down-stroke of the pick, in which the pick strikes the string with a downward attack and comes to rest on the next string.

- Rhythm: Notes should be played with a steady beat. Students are using correct counting.

- Students grasp that to "sharp" a note means to raise it one fret, and to "flat" a note means to lower it one fret. And they understand that musicians speak in terms of pitch, so that terms like "raise" and "up" mean higher in pitch, and terms like "lower" and "down" mean lower in pitch—they are not references to physical measures of distance.

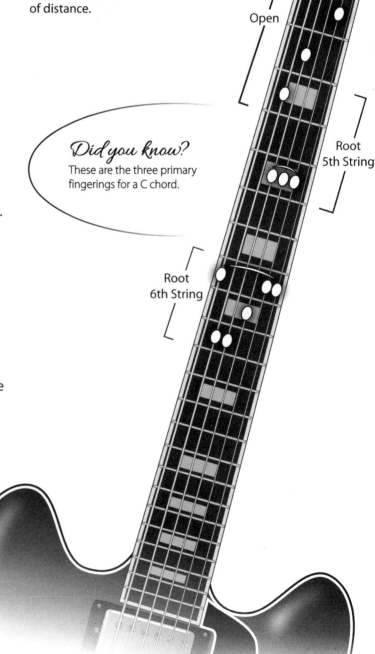

Open

Root 5th String

Did you know?
These are the three primary fingerings for a C chord.

Root 6th String

LESSON 1B (Saints and Review)

1. Line 45: MP3 track 45 is a demonstration of line 45, "When the Saints Go Marching In." Play this track for the class to prepare for learning.

2. Highlight the pickup measure. Discuss that the melody begins on beat 2 of this pick up measure.

    a. Demonstrate and count the long tied notes (bars 2–3, 4–5, etc.).

    b. Using the SI Player, set a slow playback tempo with the speed control feature and ask the class to play along.

3. Review: It is very important that the students consistently review. Remember, virtually everything the students learn in this book is a foundation technique or pattern that will be used in hundreds of variations as long as the student plays guitar. So they are not to be treated as one-off melodies to be learned and then moved beyond. Instead they are works in progress.

    a. Review "Fingerpicking Pattern No. 1" ($\frac{4}{4}$), then go over lines 26 and 28 from pages 12 and 13 of the student book.

    b. Review "Fingerpicking Pattern No. 2" ($\frac{3}{4}$), then go over lines 39 and 41 from pages 18 and 19 of the student book.

OBSERVATIONAL ASSESSMENTS

- Left hand: Fingers curved, playing on fingertips. Fingers do not interfere with adjacent strings. Thumb centered behind neck.

- Right hand: The thumb should sweep through the string, out from the guitar, towards the fingers. The fingers should remain curved and travel in an arc through the string towards the center of the palm. Thumb and fingers should remain relaxed and gently curved at all times; all motion should initiate from the knuckle joint where the fingers meet the hand, not the joint at the center of each finger.

- Students change chords on the beat (this is an intermediate- to long-term goal for absolute beginners).

INNOVATIONS @HOME

Students should be practicing at least 15 minutes per evening at home.

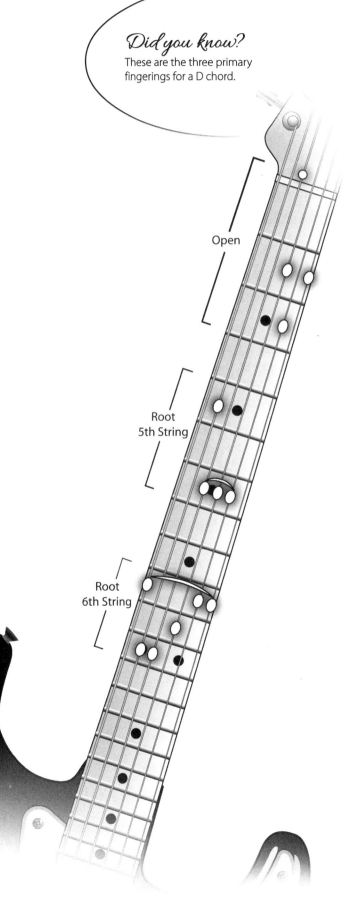

Did you know?
These are the three primary fingerings for a D chord.

Open

Root
5th String

Root
6th String

LESSON 2 | Alternate Picking, Amazing Grace

GOALS
- **Learn to read and play notes using alternate picking.**
- **Perform "Amazing Grace" as a duet using the $\frac{3}{4}$ fingerpicking pattern.**
- **Optional: Students can improvise a strum pattern using the indicated chords.**

NATIONAL STANDARDS
NS1 (Singing), **NS2** (Playing), **NS5** (Reading), **NS6** (Listening), **NS7** (Evaluating)

LESSON 2A (Alternate Picking, Page 21)

1. Introduce alternate picking, a commonly used right hand technique in which counts such as 1, 2, 3, 4 are played with a down-stroke and all the "ands" in between are played with an up-stroke.

   a. Ask students to read and study the information at the top of this page.

   b. Discuss the differences between alternate picking and the down-stroke technique we have been using.

      i. Playing by using all down-strokes is good for rock and lower bass lines, as it adds drive, rhythmic force, and a bit of attitude to the lines

      ii. Alternate picking is good for melodic lines and is the preferred technique for faster lines and melodies.

2. DVD chapter 22 gives a very good overview of alternate picking and demonstrates this technique for the "Down-Up" exercise, as does MP3 track 46. Remind students to continuously review the DVD chapters.

   a. Ask the students to play the open 1st string repeatedly with alternating down- and up-strokes.

      i. The right hand directs the pick through the string for the down-stroke, pauses and prepares to play the up-stroke. When this happens the pick just passes through the string and does not move far beyond it.

      ii. For the up-stroke, students should use a little bit of wrist movement, like turning a key, and a slight movement of the lower arm from the elbow.

      iii. Each student should take note of how well he or she is executing this technique. They can then observe and comment on other students who are close by.

   b. Repeat this practice on the open 2nd string and finally the open 3rd string. Note that when performed very rapidly, continuous alternate picking on one note produces a tremolo effect, a very common guitar technique.

   c. In line 46, alternate picking is primarily used on notes that are repeated. Use the SI Player to play MP3 track 46 at a slow tempo so the class can execute the line with a minimum amount of timing errors. Circulate throughout the class checking right hand execution and accuracy while playing the lines, and assist with any difficulties.

      i. Have the students play "Down-Up" with all down-strokes.

      ii. Have the students play "Down-Up" with alternating picking.

      iii. This exercise should help the students experience the increase in speed alternate picking allows.

3. Listen to MP3 track 47 and then ask the class to consider how the notes are organized into a sequence within this etude—four notes ascending from "do," or 1; then four notes ascending from "re," or 2; four notes ascending from "me," or 3; and, finally, four notes ascending from "fa" to "do" an octave higher. When the octave C is reached, the process is reversed—four notes down from "do" to "sol," and four notes down from "la" to "me" until the final line in the last measure, which is not a sequence.

   a. Once the sequence is understood, have the students play the first four eighth notes, repeating this several times. Then move to the next part of the sequence. Continue in this way, adding one measure at a time until the complete etude is under the students' fingers.

   b. Have them play line 47 as written. Circulate assisting as needed.

4. Optional: Ask the class to apply the chromatic scale fingering from line 33 to the two new strings.

   a. Count a slow tempo and have them play and say the chromatic scale on the 2nd string, then the 1st.

   b. Review the location of sharps and flats.

   c. Ask the class to play and say the letter names.

OBSERVATIONAL ASSESSMENTS

- Left hand: Fingers curved, playing on fingertips. Fingers do not interfere with adjacent strings. Thumb centered behind neck. Students are using one finger per fret (1–2–3–4) in the 1st position.

- Right hand: Pick is held between thumb and index finger, hand is relaxed, and all notes are played with alternate picking. When on the beat, the pick strikes the string with a downward attack, towards the floor, coming to rest halfway towards the next lower string. When on the "ands," the pick strikes the string with an upward motion, towards the ceiling, coming to rest halfway towards the next higher string.

- Rhythm: Notes should be played with a steady beat. Students are using correct counting and correct right-hand alternate picking.

LESSON 2B (Amazing Grace [duet])

1. DVD chapter 48 introduces an arrangement of "Amazing Grace." It also introduces the capo to help the students use the chords they have already learned for playing a song in practically any key.

2. Line 48: MP3 track 48 is a demonstration of line 48, "Amazing Grace." Play this track for the class to prepare for learning. Make sure they understand and can follow the first and second endings and where the forward repeat is located.

3. Discuss the pickup measure in "Amazing Grace." The melody begins on beat 3 of this pick up measure.

    a. Listen to the count off on MP3 track 48: 1–2–3–4, 1–2–PLAY. Using this count off will establish the tempo and provide the proper time to enter with the melody, whether playing or singing.

    b. Demonstrate and count the long tied notes (bars 8–9, 16–17).

    c. Using the SI Player, set a slow playback tempo with the speed control feature and ask the class to play along.

4. Optional: Reviewing helps students learn and retain the book's solid foundation of techniques and patterns that will be used in hundreds of variations for a lifetime of guitar playing.

    a. Review "Fingerpicking Pattern No. 1" ($\frac{4}{4}$), then go over lines 26 and 28 from pages 12 and 13 of the student book.

    b. Review "Fingerpicking Pattern No. 2" ($\frac{3}{4}$), then go over lines 39 and 41 from pages 18 and 19 of the student book.

OBSERVATIONAL ASSESSMENTS

• Left hand: Fingers curved, playing on fingertips. Fingers do not interfere with adjacent strings. Thumb centered behind neck.

• Right hand: The thumb should sweep through the string, out from the guitar, towards the fingers. The fingers should remain curved and travel in an arc through the string towards the center of the palm. Thumb and fingers should remain relaxed and gently curved at all times; all motion should initiate from the knuckle joint where the fingers meet the hand, not the joint at the center of each finger.

• Students change chords on the beat (this is an intermediate- to long-term goal for absolute beginners).

INNOVATIONS @HOME

• Students can look for examples of the tremolo technique with a pick (rapid alternate picking on a single note) and find examples of its use on YouTube. Some good examples are "Miserlou" as performed by Dick Dale, and the guitar solo in "Rock Around the Clock," by Bill Haley & His Comets.

• Students can also research classical guitar examples that use a specialized tremolo technique in which the thumb, p, plays a moving melody and the fingers repeat an upper note. This impressive technique imparts a feeling of sustain to a song's performance and is beyond the scope of this method, but it is exciting and worth observing and understanding. "Recuerdos de la Alhambra" is a very famous classical guitar tremolo study.

SOUND ADVICE

"Lean your body forward slightly to support the guitar against your chest, for the poetry of the music should resound in your heart."
— ANDRÉS SEGOVIA

In "Amazing Grace," students playing Guitars 2 and 3 are both playing the chords, one fingerstyle and the other strum style. Ask students to improvise some variations on the accompaniment with either pick or fingers (pick might be easier). It is important that they maintain a solid rhythm the whole time. Students using a pick to strum might want to try inserting some single-string notes in between chord strums. Students playing fingerstyle might do the opposite, interjecting a few strums with their thumb or index finger in between the fingerpicking patterns.

LESSON 3 | Flamenco Mood Ensemble

GOALS
- **Further develop the alternate picking technique.**
- **Review the Flamenco chord progression (E–F Flamenco–G Flamenco).**
- **Perform melody, harmony, and rhythm guitar.**

NATIONAL STANDARDS **NS2** (Playing), **NS5** (Reading), **NS6** (Listening), **NS7** (Evaluating), **NS8** (Making Connections)

LESSON 3A
(Flamenco Mood, Page 22)

1. Let's begin with a warm-up using line 46, on page 21 of the student book.

   a. Using the speed control in your SI Player, set a slow playback tempo for MP3 track 46, "Down-Up." Ask students to play along.

   b. Use strict alternate picking.

   c. All alternating motion should come from the wrist, not the fingers.

   d. You can also use line 47 as an excellent warm-up and alternate picking study.

2. Play MP3 track 49, "Flamenco Mood," for the class.

   a. Break the class into three groups and assign each group to Guitar 1, Guitar 2, or Guitar 3. Assign a group leader to lead individual practice sessions as you circulate assisting as needed.

   b. When students are ready, they can either break into small ensembles or stay in their sections to begin rehearsing as one big ensemble.

   c. Students can play along with the MP3 track. Note that by using the SI player you can slow the track down and mute Guitars 1 and 2, leaving only the rhythm guitar part.

   d. It is important that students learn to play all three parts. We want to encourage them to experience playing melody, harmony, and rhythm guitar. So throughout this unit return to this song with students changing parts.

OBSERVATIONAL ASSESSMENTS

- Are students able to keep good time and stay together as an ensemble? Especially listen for timing issues between Guitar 1 (eighth notes) and Guitar 2 (quarter and half notes).

- When playing the Guitar 2 part, students need to be aware of the G♯ (1st fret, 3rd string).

- Discuss the accent marks (measures 11–13) and the ritardondo in the final bar.

LESSON 3B
(Review Amazing Grace
and Flamenco Mood, Pages 21 and 22)

1. Let's begin with a warm-up using line 47, page 21. This is a great alternate picking/string crossing study. In other words, in addition to strict alternate picking it requires the student to cross from string to string. The four-note scale pattern that is the basis of this etude is also an excellent pattern that can be used in improvised guitar solos.

   a. Using the speed control in your SI Player set a slow playback tempo for MP3 track 47, "Scale Etude." Ask students to play along.

   b. Use strict alternate picking. The down–up pattern does not change when crossing strings.

   c. All alternating motion should come from the wrist, not the fingers.

2. Revisit "Amazing Grace," on page 21.

   a. Ask the students to break into groups to rehearse "Amazing Grace." Each student should be assigned to Guitar 1 (melody), Guitar 2 (fingerpicking accompaniment) or Guitar 3 (strumming accompaniment).

   b. All students should perform **all three** parts, so this is an opportunity to switch the parts around if they have not done so yet.

   c. Students can play along with the CD track in groups or as a class.

SOUND ADVICE

Students playing Guitar 2 and Guitar 3 are both playing the chords, one fingerstyle and the other strum style. Ask students to improvise some variations on the accompaniment with either pick or fingers (pick might be easier). It is important that they maintain a solid rhythm the whole time. Students using a pick to strum might want to try inserting some single-string notes in between chord strums. Students playing fingerstyle might do the opposite, interjecting a few strums with their thumb or index finger in between the fingerpicking patterns.

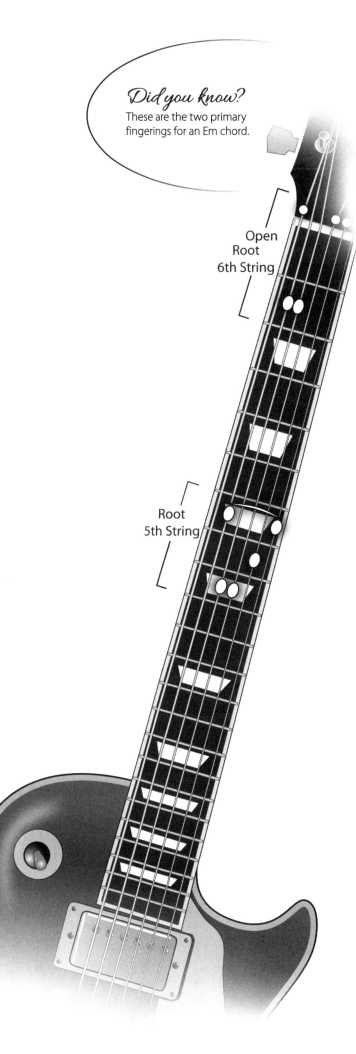

Did you know?
These are the two primary fingerings for an Em chord.

Open
Root
6th String

Root
5th String

LESSON 4 | Ode to Joy and Chromatic Strength Builder

 GOALS
- **Introduce the dotted eighth note.**
- **Review the chord progression in the key of G (G, D, Em).**
- **Perform melody, harmony, and rhythm guitar.**
- **Use all six strings in a strength-building chromatic exercise.**

NATIONAL STANDARDS   **NS2** (Playing), **NS5** (Reading), **NS6** (Listening), **NS7** (Evaluating), **NS9** (History & Culture)

LESSON 4A (Ode to Joy, Page 23)

1. DVD chapter 24 introduces "Ode to Joy" and counting the dotted quarter note as does MP3 track 50. Use these resources to prepare the class.

   a. Review the song form—follow the first and second endings.

   b. Explain and discuss the dotted quarter note. A dot adds half of the original value to a note. So a dotted quarter note is the equivalent of three eighth notes tied together.

   c. Using the SI Player to loop measure 4 from "Ode to Joy," have the students practice the dotted quarter note rhythm with correct picking by until they become familiar with it.

   d. Students should give the dotted quarter note its full rhythmic value.

   e. Students should use an up-stroke for the eighth note that follows the dotted quarter.

2. Rehearse "Ode to Joy," making sure the class has listened to the piece several times using the DVD or MP3 track before attempting it. It would be good to play the recording three times, asking the class to follow the music and focus their ears on one guitar part at a time through the entire song.

   a. Break the class into groups and assign each group to Guitar 1, Guitar 2, or Guitar 3. Assign a group leader to lead individual practice sessions as you circulate assisting as needed.

   b. When students are ready, they can either break into small ensembles or stay in their sections to begin rehearsing as one big ensemble.

   c. Students can play along with the MP3 track. Note that by using the SI Player you can slow the track down and mute Guitars 1 and 2, leaving only the rhythm guitar part.

   d. It is important that students learn to play all three parts. We want to encourage them to experience playing melody, harmony, and rhythm guitar. So throughout this unit return to this song with students changing parts.

OBSERVATIONAL ASSESSMENTS

Are students able to keep good time and stay together as an ensemble? Especially listen for timing issues between Guitar 1 (dotted quarter–eighth notes, measures 4, 5, and 13) and Guitar 2 (dotted quarter–eighth notes; measures 4, 5, and 13).

LESSON 4B (Review Amazing Grace and Flamenco Mood, Pages 21 and 22)

1. Let's begin with a warm-up using line 47 on page 21 of the student book. This is a great alternate picking/string crossing study. In other words, in addition to strict alternate picking it requires the student to cross from string to string. The four-note scale pattern that is the basis of this etude is also an excellent pattern that can be used in improvised guitar solos.

   a. Using the speed control in the SI Player set a slow playback tempo for MP3 track 47, "Scale Etude." Ask students to play-along.

   b. Use strict alternate picking. The pattern of down–up does not change when crossing strings.

   c. All alternating motion should come from the wrist, not the fingers.

2. Review "Amazing Grace," on page 21.

   a. Ask the students to break into groups to rehearse "Amazing Grace." Each student should be assigned to Guitar 1 (melody), Guitar 2 (fingerpicking accompaniment), or Guitar 3 (strumming accompaniment).

   b. All students should perform **all three** parts, so this is an opportunity to switch the parts around if they have not done so yet.

   c. Students can play in groups or as a class along with the CD track.

3. Review "Flamenco Mood," page 22.

a. Ask the students to break into groups to rehearse "Flamenco Mood." Each student should be assigned to Guitar 1 (melody), Guitar 2 (counter-melody) or Guitar 3 (strumming accompaniment). Again, it would be good to listen first to the song three times. Each time the students should focus their attention on only one guitar part to pick it out from the mix.

b. All students should perform **all three** parts, so this is an opportunity to switch the parts around if they have not done so yet.

c. Students can play in groups or as a class along with the CD track.

SOUND ADVICE

*"Nothing is more beautiful
    than the sound of the guitar,
            save perhaps two."*

— F. CHOPIN

Students playing guitars 1 and 2 are playing the melody (Guitar 1) and counter melody (Guitar 2). It is important that they maintain appropriate rhythm the whole time and execute the dotted quarter notes correctly. Students playing accompaniment (Guitar 3) will need to control their volume so that they do not overpower the first two guitars. If this is the case usually the performance will be balanced. As a rule of thumb, if you can only hear your part and not the others, you are playing too loud.

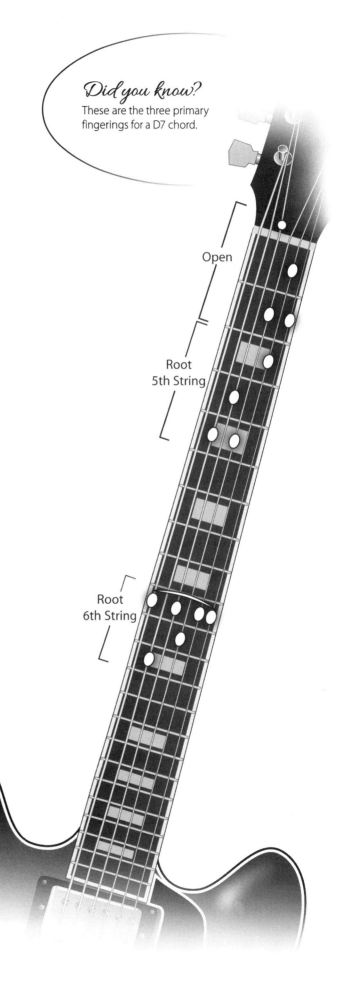

Did you know?
These are the three primary fingerings for a D7 chord.

Open

Root
5th String

Root
6th String

LESSON 5 | The One Grip Blues

 GOALS
- **Learn a fundamental blues pattern.**
- **Improvise using a stylistically appropriate blues pattern.**
- **Perform in a blues-rock style playing both lead and rhythm parts.**

 NATIONAL STANDARDS **NS2** (Playing), **NS3** (Improvising), **NS5** (Reading), **NS6** (Listening), **NS7** (Evaluating)

TEACHER NOTE
(The One-Grip Blues Pattern, Page 25)

Improvising is not just making stuff up in the moment with a minor pentatonic scale. It's best for students to have a few tools at their disposal such as a few pre-determined, stylistically appropriate patterns known as "licks." Those licks, combined with a scale pattern or two and a chord shape or two provide almost infinite possibilities for improvisation. Think of improvising as a type of spontaneous re-organization of pre-determined ideas. The following explanation is for teachers. Students do not need to know the theory behind this new lick, but it may be useful for you as an instructor.

Why does moving one simple two-note "grip" one fret allow it to work over the IV and V chords? Let's look at this from two perspectives.

1. First, just the physical guitar pattern point of view: Here are standard chord forms for A7, D7, and E7. You can immediately see that the top two notes in the A7 chord are one fret above the top two voices in the D7 and one fret below the top two voices for E7.

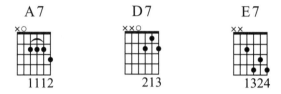

2. Now, from a theory standpoint: The two most important notes in a dominant seventh chord are the 3rd and 7th, because those are the notes that give the chord its characteristic sound.

The 3rd and 7th of A7 are C♯ and G
The 7th and 3rd of D7 are C and F♯
The 7th and 3rd of E7 are D and G♯

Take a look at the diagram below. You can see that moving the 3rd and 7th of the A7 down one fret (a half step) creates the 7th and 3rd of D7, and moving the 3rd and 7th of the A7 up one fret creates the 7th and 3rd of E7.

This concept can be applied to a blues in **any** key. For example, to apply it to a blues in B♭ everything moves up one fret. A blues in the key of B would be two frets higher, and so on.

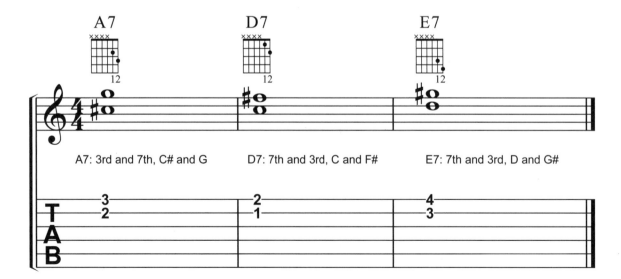

LESSON 5A (The One-Grip Blues Pattern, Page 25)

1. DVD chapter 25 is a complete demonstration and explanation of this important blues pattern. Students should watch chapter 25 and chapter 26 (a full performance) so they have an idea of the musical sound and goal of the lesson before they play.

a. Direct students to line 52. "The One-Grip Blues Pattern" is a two-note chord fingering on the 1st and 2nd strings. For A7 the grip is at the 2nd fret, for D7 it is at the 1st fret, and for E7 it is at the 3rd fret.

b. Play MP3 track 55 for the class. It is a 12-bar blues in A with an intro. They should play along using the one-grip pattern—changing between A7, D7, and E7 at the appropriate times.

c. Play MP3 track 54 for the class. Students should learn both Guitar 1 and Guitar 2.

i. Guitar 2 is based on the blues progression learned on page 16 of the student book. The lead guitar part (Guitar 1) is based on the one-grip blues pattern.

ii. The song starts with a classic blues introduction. Students should memorize this pattern—they can use it to start any blues in the key of A. Bars 13 and 14 (first ending) feature a classic blues **turnaround**, which comes at the end of the 12 bar blues progression and sets it up to repeat. The turnaround is a two-bar melody that makes the music feel like it isn't done, but instead turns it around to begin the progression again. Measures 13 and 15 (second ending) use the same turnaround lick, but it is altered to signal an end to the song instead of a return to the beginning.

iii. Chord frames are not indicated throughout the rhythm guitar part (Guitar 2). Typically, just the basic names of the chords (A7, D7, and E7) are indicated, and it's assumed the guitarist knows to play the boogie pattern or one of its variations.

iv. On the recording, the lead guitarist improvises a solo on the repeat based on the optional slide and hammer licks learned on the previous page. Once students are comfortable playing the entire song, they may want to experiment with improvising blues solos over the recorded rhythm on track 55.

SOUND SUGGESTIONS

• Locate some recordings of authentic blues guitar or find some vintage footage on YouTube.

• Rhythm is the key to improvised guitar solos—perhaps more than notes. Play the backing track and ask a student to tap out a forceful rhythmic idea on the desk. Once they have the rhythm in their head ask them to apply it to the one-grip pattern.

• Call and response: Ask students to "trade fours"—one student improvises for the first four bars then the next student jumps in, hopefully picking up on the idea or rhythm played by the first student. This can go round and round.

LESSON 5B
(Advanced Optional Lead Guitar Variation, Page 25)

1. Students who can play the basic one-grip pattern with confidence and are looking for a challenge can try this advanced variation. It uses two critical lead guitar techniques: slides and hammer-ons. It is demonstrated in DVD chapter 25 and MP3 track 53.

a. First, students place their hands in the two-finger grip position for A7 on the first two strings. Next, have them drop down one fret, play the 1st-fret C, and then *slide* up to the 2nd-fret C♯. The C♯ should be sounded by the force of the finger sliding up from C. Next have them play the 1st-string G. The left hand should always remain in the basic two-finger grip position.

b. For the D7 chord, students play the open B, and then *hammer* the 1st finger down onto the C with enough force to sound the note. Then they should play the F♯ with the 2nd finger.

c. For the E7 chord, start on the 2nd-fret C♯, and have them slide up exactly as they did for the A7 chord.

> **Note** *This lick is based on a tri-tone interval (♯4th), which is more than the students should know right now. However, the inversion of the tri-tone is just up the neck six frets. So a variation can be played by moving the three chord pattern up the neck: A7 at the 8th fret, D7 at the 7th fret, and E7 at the 9th fret. For even more variety try moving back and forth between the positions.*

OBSERVATIONAL ASSESSMENTS

• Students are counting and playing the melody with correct timing. Especially pay attention to the tied notes in bars 4 and 5.

• Chords are changing on the correct beat.

• Students are using a solid rhythm whether strumming or fingerpicking. Important: The accompaniment part provides the rhythmic foundation. It is not just a series of notes. Without strong rhythm it will not work.

SOUND ADVICE

"Nobody loves me but my mother, and she could be jivin' too."

— B.B. KING

INNOVATIONS @HOME

Ask students to practice "One-Grip Blues" at home with track 54 and to practice improvising along with track 55.

SOUND EXPECTATIONS

• After a week of practice students should be able to perform both the Guitar 1 and Guitar 2 guitar parts to "One-Grip Blues" with reasonable accuracy, in time, and with few mistakes.

• Students should be attempting to improvise guitar solos using the one-grip pattern. A perfect performance would be to always change patterns with the chords, play rhythmically strong phrases, and make clear musical statements. A "needs significant improvement" assessment would be not being able to follow the chord progression.

LESSON 6 | Review and Assessment

GOALS
- Students will review key songs.
- Perform etudes and ensembles that include accented notes, tied notes, pick up measures, and chromatic runs.
- Students will solidify notes on the 1st, 2nd, 3rd, and 4th strings and chords learned to date, including C, G, D, E, F Flamenco, G Flamenco, Em, A7, D7, and E7.

- Students will review alternate picking, fingerpicking, and strum patterns.
- Assess student progress and determine individual needs and goals for progress.

NATIONAL STANDARDS NS1 (Singing), NS2 (Playing), NS3 (Improvising), NS4 (Composing), NS5 (Reading), NS6 (Listening), NS7 (Evaluating), NS8 (Making Connections), NS9 (History & Culture)

LESSON 6A: REVIEW AND OBSERVATIONAL ASSESSMENT (Page 20)

1. Review and assess Lesson 1A (Notes on the 2nd and 1st Strings, Page 20)

   a. Ask the class to perform line 43, "Notes on the 1st and 2nd Strings," and scan the class for left and right hand position and technique. Who looks good and who needs help?

   b. Are students able to maintain a steady beat? Can they say the note names out loud as they play?

2. Review and assess "Jingle Bells" and "When the Saints Go Marching In" (page 20)

   a. Line 44: Ask the class to look at the music. What do they notice about the road map they will follow? Discuss how first and second endings work in "Jingle Bells."

   b. Play MP3 track 44 and have the students perform at an appropriate tempo selected with the SI Player.

   c. Ask the class to perform the music and scan the class for left and right hand position and technique. Who looks good and who needs help?

   d. Are students able to maintain a steady beat?

   e. Left and right hand position: who looks good and who needs help?

   f. Line 45: "When the Saints Go Marching In" (page 20). Ask the class which string or strings are used exclusively for the melody.

   g. Are the students holding the tied notes for their full value?

   h. Can the students play the melody without altering the tempo with the SI Player?

LESSON 6B: REVIEW AND OBSERVATIONAL ASSESSMENT (Page 21)

1. Review alternate picking. Observe the class as they perform line 46, "Down-Up," and for each student make note:

   a. Left and right hand position: who looks good and who needs help?

   b. Are students able to maintain a steady pulse when using alternate picking? Who needs assistance with this right hand technique? Is the student using alternate picking or random variations?

   c. Are students able to count and feel the eighth note pulse while playing steady eighth notes? Can the students say "down, up" mimicking his or her right hand while performing line 46?

2. Review and assess line 47, "Scale Etude" (page 21). Ask the class to practice line 47. Students should assist each other when possible. Observe the class and for each student make note:

   a. Left and right hand position: who looks good and who needs help?

   b. Are students able to maintain a steady beat, moving smoothly from string to string with alternate picking?

3. Review and assess line 48, "Amazing Grace (duet)" (page 21).

   a. Can students accurately play the melody? Were the pickup notes executed properly?

   b. Who needs assistance with the fingerpicking pattern and who needs help with making the chord changes?

   c. Is there a nice blend between guitar parts? Are there dynamics? Ask the students to mark in a specific measure to switch to palm muting.

   d. Optional: Are students able to play and sing at a medium tempo?

LESSON 6C: REVIEW AND OBSERVATIONAL ASSESSMENT (Page 22)

1. Have the students play "Flamenco Mood."

   a. Can students use the correct right hand technique, with alternate picking for the eighth notes, and stay in time?

   b. Who needs assistance with the melody or countermelody?

   c. Are students able to count and feel the quarter note pulse with the right hand?

   d. Can students successfully read the accidentals in the music?

   e. Have the students successfully applied the ritardando to the final measure for all parts?

   f. Is there a good blend and feel between the parts?

LESSON 6D: REVIEW AND OBSERVATIONAL ASSESSMENT (Page 23)

1. Review the chords G, D, and Em

   a. Can the students visualize these chords?

   b. Can the students switch chords with the fingers moving as a unit, not one finger at a time?

   c. Can the students improvise a strum using just the chord symbols above the melody?

2. Review and assess line 50, "Ode to Joy."

   a. Can students correctly play the melody?

   b. Identify who needs assistance with the melody and who needs help with the fingerpicking pattern.

   c. Are students able to count and feel the dotted quarter note pulse while playing the melody (Guitar 1) and countermelody (Guitar 2)?

   d. Is there a nice blend between guitar parts? Ask the students to switch parts. How well do they perform the new part?

LESSON 6E: REVIEW AND OBSERVATIONAL ASSESSMENT (Pages 25, 26, and 27)

1. Review DVD chapter 25 for the one-grip blues patterns.

   a. Can the students visualize and perform these two-note grips?

   b. Can the student switch grips with the fingers moving as a unit, not one finger at a time? As these are one-grip blues patterns, make sure they use all down-strokes.

   c. Review MP3 track 53 to revisit the slide and hammer-on techniques presented in the method.

   d. Once these one-grip patterns are under the students' fingers with the written rhythms, can they improvise a new rhythm?

2. Review the information at the top of page 26 and play MP3 track 54 for "One-Grip Blues."

   a. Can the students correctly follow the form indications (i.e., the road map) for "One-Grip Blues?"

   b. Are the students using the correct fingerings and playing in the 2nd position for Guitar 1 and Guitar 2?

   c. Have the students practiced and become familiar with the introduction in measures 1 and 2 and can they perform it together accurately?

   d. If you have a student that can improvise a blues solo in A, add them into the mix after the first repeat.

   e. Ask for volunteers to improvise new rhythms for the Guitar 1 grips.

LESSON 6F: FORMAL ASSESSMENTS FOR LEVEL 3

1. Students will form into groups/ensembles with one person to each part. Each ensemble will select one of the following pieces to perform for the class. The students will pick a name for their ensemble and announce it to the class before performing their selection. There are significant differences in difficulty, however, the critical element is how musically the students perform and present their selected song.

   a. "Amazing Grace (duet)" (page 21): Perform as written or (optionally) with vocals. If performing with vocals and capos are available, have the students use the same chord shapes but find an appropriate key for them to sing in.

   b. "Flamenco Mood" (page 22): Make sure to grade appropriately for the accented notes and the ritardando.

   c. "Ode to Joy" (page 23): Make sure to grade appropriately for the correct dotted quarter note values.

   d. "One-Grip Blues" (pages 26 and 27). You might ask students to improvise guitar solos on the repeat.

2. Use Worksheet #15 to grade student performance. You may also distribute Worksheet #15a to the class so they can create their own peer evaluations.

   a. As the students perform, look at their technique:

      i. Chords are clear, all notes ring clearly without any muffled or muted strings.

      ii. Pick is held between the thumb and 1st finger.

      iii. Fingerpicking patterns use the correct right-hand approach.

   b. As the students perform, look at their musical skills:

      i. Accuracy in the rhythms.

      ii. Notes and chords are correct.

      iii. Performances have a steady tempo.

      iv. Appropriate musicality is presented, such as dynamics and accents.

Make sure the students understand that the more they practice the easier it will become to play the guitar. With practice the technical challenges become more familiar and the students can focus on other important aspects of music such as feeling, dynamics, and interpretation.

LESSON 1 | Basic Theory, I–V7, Playing by Ear

GOALS
- Students will discuss and listen for basic chord quality: major, minor, and dominant seventh.
- Students will learn G7.
- Students will learn to identify the I and the V7 chords of a key.

NATIONAL STANDARDS **NS1** (Singing), **NS2** (Playing), **NS5** (Reading), **NS6** (Listening), **NS7** (Evaluating), **NS8** (Making Connections)

LESSON 1A (I–V7, Pages 28–29)

1. Review the explanation of chord symbol notation at the top of page 28 of the student book.

2. On the guitar, or at the piano, play major, minor, and dominant seventh chords for the class. Ask the students to identify each chord as major, minor, or dominant seventh. Discuss and provide advice for identifying the sound quality differences between each type of chord.

3. Line 56: Students will practice line 56. Stop them on a G7 chord and discuss how the G7 seems to want to resolve back to the C chord. This is a good opportunity to discuss tension and release.

4. Technique tip: The same three fingers in roughly the same shape are used to play both C and G7. To make changing between the two chords easier, have the students

   a. Play C, then spread their fingers outward from the inside strings towards the outer strings to play the G7.

   b. Now have them play the G7 then contract the fingers towards the middle strings to play the C chord.

5. Use DVD chapter 27 to reinforce.

LESSON 1B (I–V7, Pages 28–29)

1. Write out a C major scale on the white board (see top of page 29 of the student book).

   a. Ask the class to sing the scale using solfege syllables: do–re–mi–fa–sol–la–ti–do

   b. Try other starting pitches and sing the major scale from each one. Discuss that the major scale is always relative, or the same. Regardless of the names of the pitches, the basic major scale sound (do–re–me …) remains.

   c. Next repeat the process using numbers instead of pitches: 1–2–3–4–5–6–7–8. So all we are doing is substituting numbers for the solfege syllables.

   d. Try this from various pitches. Again, point out how each scale is relatively the same. Note to the class how the scale resolves on "8."

2. Now play a C chord and assist the students in singing C–G–C, then replace the letter names with do–sol–do, and finally with 1–5–1.

3. Write several major scales on the white board (a few are provided below). Ask the class to count up from the first note in each scale and indentify the I and the V for each.

   G major: G–A–B–C–D–E–F♯–G
   A major: A–B–C♯–D–E–F♯–G♯–A
   F major: F–G–A–B♭–C–D–E–F
   E♭ major: E♭–F–G–A♭–B♭–C–D–E♭

LESSON 1C (Playing by Ear, Page 29)

1. Play DVD chapter 28 for the class.

2. Distribute Worksheet #16. These are the lyrics for "He's Got the Whole World in His Hands."

3. This song uses just two chords: the I chord (C) and the V7 chord (G7). The starting chord (C) is provided above the lyrics. Together, the class will identify all the rest of the chord changes and mark each one above the correct syllable on their handouts. There are several methods for doing this:

   a. You can begin on the C chord and sing aloud. Do not change chords—ask the class to raise their hands when it sounds bad. Do this several times until they indentify the exact word or syllable where the chord begins to clash—that is where the chord should change to G7. Continue this process throughout the song, remembering that the correct chord will always be either C or G7. Write the chord symbols above the words.

   b. Alternatively, you could listen to the song with guitar accompaniment on the CD, then play along with the minus guitar version (track 60), asking the students to identify when to change chords.

   c. Students can also work individually, strumming and singing the song softly and identifying on the worksheet when to change chords.

SOUND ADVICE

This is not a competition and it will be a very foreign skill to the class. However, it can be a lot of fun and very exciting. It is critical for no one to think they can't do it just because they didn't get it right away. Keep it fun. Laugh off the mistakes—they will happen. It is important to encourage the students to begin listening in this very subjective manner and for them to realize that because the chord progressions to all songs are *so* repetitive and similar, over time, and with practice, they will be able to identify these types of things pretty easily by ear—especially the extremely common progressions like I–V–I, I–IV–V, I–vi–IV–V, etc.

OBSERVATIONAL ASSESSMENTS

• Can students easily relate scale tones (C–D–E–F–G–A–B–C) with their numeric counterparts (1–8)?

• When attempting to decide between the I and the V chord students are listening for the clash between the melody and the current chord.

INNOVATIONS @HOME

Assign a song from the following list of two-chord songs that all begin on the C chord. You can download the free reproducible lyric worksheets (#s 17–24) for each song at www.alfred.com/SoundInnovations/SIGuitar. Ask students to sing the songs at home and use the processes described in class to decide when to change from C to G7.

"Down in the Valley"
"My Darlin' Clementine"
"Farmer in the Dell"
"Mary Had a Little Lamb"
"Merrily We Roll Along"
"Polly Wolly Doodle"
"Shoo Fly, Don't Bother Me"
"Three Blind Mice"

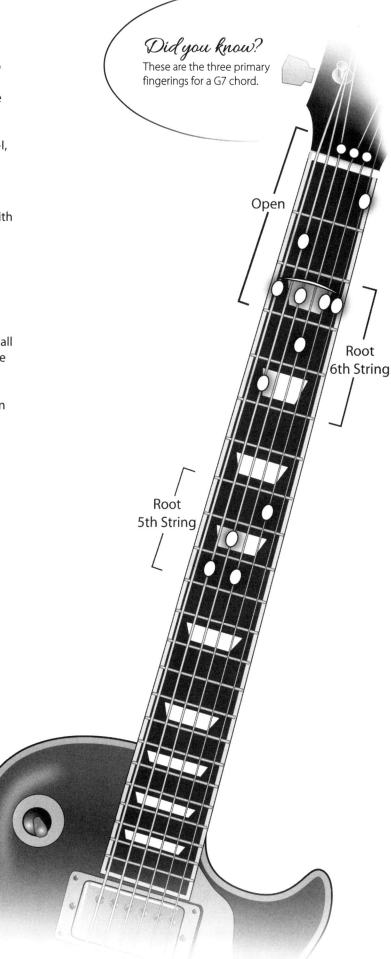

Did you know? These are the three primary fingerings for a G7 chord.

Open

Root 6th String

Root 5th String

LESSON 2 | Simple Gifts

 GOALS
- **Students will perform a guitar arrangement of "Simple Gifts," a Shaker tune composed in 1848. This melody has been used as a theme by the great American composer Aaron Copland in "Appalachian Spring" and "Old American Song," and a modern treatment by the rock band Weezer exists in their song "The Greatest Man That Ever Lived."**
- **Students will perform "Simple Gifts" in a duo or optional trio setting, playing both the melody and accompaniment parts.**

- **Students will apply standard guitar chord forms to the $\frac{4}{4}$ fingerpicking accompaniment, illustrating how all pieces of music, even classical pieces, use similar basic chord structures.**
- **Students will follow performance directives such as *Coda* (⊕) and *D.S. al Coda*.**
- **Students will improvise a strum accompaniment based on the indicated chords.**

 NATIONAL STANDARDS **NS1** (Singing), **NS2** (Playing), **NS5** (Reading), **NS6** (Listening)

LESSON 2A (Simple Gifts, Pages 30–31)

1. MP3 track 61 contains a full performance of this song. Keep in mind that you can use the SI Player to isolate either guitar part, and slow down and loop sections for practice.

   a. Begin with a review and demonstration of Guitar 1, the melody. This part is very simple and diatonic, but the students need to pay careful attention to the mixed rhythms: eighth, quarter, dotted quarter, and half notes.

   b. Use the SI Player to slow the tempo down and ask the class to perform the melody in unison using the MP3 track as an accompaniment.

   c. Discuss and review the song form making sure the students are aware of the *D.S.* sign at measure 2, and where the performer is directed to go to the *Coda* (⊕) at the end of measure 7.

2. Make sure that the bass notes are accurately articulated by the students with their thumbs. The students can begin by playing only the bass notes, on beats 1 and 3, along with the recording. This will help to make them familiar and comfortable with changing between strings for the bass notes. It will also increase their awareness of the chord changes.

3. Next add the fingers (*i–m–a*), completing the fingerpicking pattern.

4. A third part can be created by incorporating the indicated Guitar 3 strum pattern. Keep in mind when using the up-strum with this accompaniment pattern that you do not have to strike all the strings, but only the two or three closest to the floor.

OBSERVATIONAL ASSESSMENTS

- Students are counting and playing the melody with correct timing.
- Chords are changing on the correct beat.
- Students are listening and trying to blend the parts into a whole.
- Students are following the accidentals carefully and using the indicated picking.

INNOVATIONS @HOME

Ask students to research the Shaker song "Simple Gifts" online. Find recorded versions of the original Copland work and locate arrangements for other instruments and historical insights to this piece. A great resource is AmericanMusicPreservation.com.

SOUND ADVICE

"To stop the flow of music would be like the stopping of time itself, incredible and inconceivable."

— AARON COPLAND

LESSON 2B (Playing by Ear, More Two-Chord Songs)

1. Ask the students to choose one or several songs from the following list of two-chord songs.

   "Down in the Valley"
   "My Darlin' Clementine"
   "Farmer in the Dell"
   "Mary Had a Little Lamb"
   "Merrily We Roll Along"
   "Polly Wolly Doodle"
   "Shoo Fly, Don't Bother Me"
   "Three Blind Mice"

2. Download the free reproducible lyric worksheets for each song (#s 17–24) at www.alfred.com/SoundInnovations/SIGuitar. Ask students to sing the song while you play the chords on your guitar or piano.

3. Ask the students to count while you play the song and have them determine the time signature, either $\frac{3}{4}$ or $\frac{4}{4}$.

4. You can have the class raise their hands each time they feel the chord should change.

5. When the correct chords are determined, have the students write the appropriate chords on the chord sheets and sing and play.

6. Keep in mind that this is a great way to develop the students' ears and repertoire.

LESSON 3 | Für Elise

GOALS
- Students will perform a guitar rendition of "Für Elise," originally written for fortepiano (the predecessor to the modern piano) by Beethoven
- Students will perform "Für Elise" in a duo setting, playing both the melody and accompaniment parts
- Students will apply standard guitar chord forms to the accompaniment, illustrating how all pieces of music, even classical pieces, use similar basic chord structures
- Students will follow performance directives such as "rit" and "a tempo"
- Students will improvise a fingerstyle accompaniment based on the indicated chords

NATIONAL STANDARDS NS2 (Playing), NS5 (Reading), NS6 (Listening), NS7 (Evaluating), NS8 (Making Connections), NS9 (History & Culture)

LESSON 3A (Für Elise, Guitar 1, Pages 32–33)

1. Let's begin with a warm-up using line 46, on page 21 of the student book.

   a. Using the speed control in your SI Player, set a slow playback tempo for MP3 track 46, "Down-Up." Ask students to play-along.

   b. Use strict alternate picking.

   c. All alternating motion should come from the wrist, not the fingers.

   d. You can also use line 47 as an excellent warm-up and alternate picking study.

2. Play DVD chapter 29 for the class. MP3 track 62 contains a full performance of the music. Remember that by using the SI Player, you can isolate either guitar, and slow down and loop sections for practice.

3. Begin with a review and demonstration of Guitar 1, the melody. This part is very chromatic so students need to pay careful attention to the accidentals.

4. Ask the class to perform the melody in unison using the CD as an accompaniment. Use the SI Player to slow the tempo down.

5. Discuss and review the song form (first and second endings), the ritardando at bar 16, and the "a tempo" on the pickup to bar 18. You will need to conduct through this section.

   Note *In the opening chromatic phrase (E–D♯–E–D♯) the open E string needs to be silenced as the D♯ is played. Allowing it to ring into the D♯ will produce a rather ugly sound.*

LESSON 3B (Für Elise, Guitar 2, Pages 32–33)

1. Use either the DVD or the CD and ask the students to pay careful attention to the Guitar 2 part. You can use the SI Player to isolate Guitar 2, making it much easier to hear.

   a. Review the chords for the part: Am–E7–C–G/B. Explain that G/B is just the middle four strings of the standard G chord form.

   b. Ask the class to play the Guitar 2 part in unison using the CD as accompaniment. Use the SI Player to slow the tempo down.

2. Once students are comfortable with both parts, split the class into two groups (or several duos) and ask them to begin practicing the piece as a duet.

3. Circulate throughout helping as needed.

4. Ask the class to switch parts.

LESSON 3C
(Für Elise, Fingerpicking Guitar, Pages 32–33)

1. Ask the class to apply the $\frac{3}{4}$ fingerpicking pattern (see page 18 of the student book) to the chords of this piece.

2. Again break into two groups. One group plays Guitar 1 and the other should improvise a fingerpicking accompaniment using the indicated chords, based mainly on "Fingerpicking Pattern No. 2."

3. Ask the class to switch parts.

OBSERVATIONAL ASSESSMENTS

- Students are counting and playing the melody with correct timing.
- Chords are changing on the correct beat.
- Students are listening and trying to blend the parts into a whole.
- Students are following the accidentals carefully and using the indicated picking.

INNOVATIONS @HOME

Ask students to research Beethoven or "Für Elise" online. Find recorded versions of the original piano piece and locate arrangements performed on other instruments.

LESSON 4 | Swing Feel and When the Saints Go Marchin' In

GOALS
- Students will be introduced to the swing feel, traditional jazz, and blue notes.
- Students will perform "When the Saints Go Marchin' In" in a trio setting, playing the melody, counter melody, and accompaniment.
- Students will review the G, D, C, and G7 chords and add a new standard guitar chord form, D7, to their basic chord vocabulary.
- Students will follow performance directives such as "staccato" and "accented staccato" (with accents on beats 3 and 4).

NATIONAL STANDARDS NS2 (Playing), NS5 (Reading), NS6 (Listening), NS7 (Evaluating), NS8 (Making Connections), NS9 (History & Culture)

LESSON 4A
(Traditional Jazz and the Swing Feel, Page 34)

1. Begin by introducing the class to traditional jazz, which evolved early in the 1900s in New Orleans.

   a. This lively and upbeat style grew from the practice of having several members of a band simultaneously improvise elaborate melody variations and counter melody lines that weave around the basic melody. These performers played with an uneven interpretation of the eighth note that we now call "swing feel."

   b. Early recordings of traditional jazz often featured a banjo. Its loud, bright tone recorded well and cut through the horn section better than the mellower guitar. But both were common rhythm section instruments.

   c. The introduction of the electric guitar, with its added volume, brought the guitar to the forefront as a lead instrument within the jazz band, since it could now compete with the much louder horns. Benny Goodman famously broke new ground when he racially integrated his band, bringing in Charlie Christian, the man many consider to be the father of modern jazz guitar. During his short life, Charlie Christian inspired many of the great jazz guitarists that followed: Wes Montgomery, George Benson, Les Paul, and Kenny Burrell, to name a few.

2. Swing overview: Swing is a specific way eighth notes are interpreted in jazz. Early jazz set itself apart from folk and classical music by interpreting the eighth-note melodies unevenly, or more to the point, long–short.

   a. Be aware that straight and swing eighth notes are written exactly the same.

   b. The swing feel is often stated to have a "gallop."

   c. Tip: Although we call it "long–short," a good swing feel comes from feeling the short note fall **into** the next long note, so after the first long note it's "short–long, short–long," and so on, with a galloping kind of rhythm.

3. Along with the overview of the swing feel, play MP3 track 63 to prepare the students for playing lines 63 and 64 on page 34 of the student book. The track demonstrates each example played straight and then with a swing feel.

   a. For even eighth note rhythms, have the students say "1 and 2 and 3 and 4 and." For uneven eighth note rhythms, have the students say "1 uh 2 uh 3 uh 4 uh." Students should count aloud along with the examples on tracks 63 and 64.

   b. When the students are familiar with saying the rhythm syllables, have them play along with MP3 track 63.

   c. Repeat the rhythm of line 63 only on the open 3rd string, G.

   d. Repeat this again and this time play all of the same rhythms using only the open 1st string, E.

   e. Ask the class if they are comfortable playing the swing feel and if they understand it is a feel and interpretation, not something written in the staff.

4. Line 64: "Swing Example No. 2." Using the speed control in your SI Player set a slow playback tempo for MP3 track 64. Ask students to play-along.

   a. Swing eighths are to be performed using strict alternate picking.

   b. All alternating motion should come from the wrist and elbow, not the fingers.

   c. This example will help students with phrasing in the next ensemble piece, "When the Saints Go Marchin' In."

LESSON 4B
(When the Saints Go Marchin' In, Pages 34–35)

1. Play DVD chapter 31 for the class. MP3 track 65 contains a special overview of the rhythm guitar part.

   a. Pay close attention to the DVD explanation and how the staccato and staccato accent will keep the chords from ringing but will accent beats 2 and 4, just like the hi-hat does in a jazz drummer's kit.

   b. The rhythm guitar is muted by lightly touching the strings with the right palm after a strum. Students should simply collapse the wrist and touch the strings to quickly mute them, then prepare to strum the accented staccato with more energy, then again collapse the wrist and touch the strings with the palm, and repeat this process.

   c. Have the entire class practice this technique

2. The "blue notes" used in this ensemble are another aspect of blues and jazz that set it apart from folk and classical music. Blue notes are dissonant notes that early blues singers used to bring a grittier feel to the music. "Saints" uses two blue notes from the key of G: B♭ and F. (See below for an illustration of these notes.) These are the flatted 3rd and 7th notes, but students don't need to know this at the moment. They *should* know that by adding these two notes to our note choices we impart an obviously blues-like sound quality.

   a. Shift to 2nd position to play the counter melody in bar 8. Shifting positions is a technique that many professional guitarists use to make a phrase or lick easier and more finger-friendly when performing a song or improvising.

   b. Have the students listen for the blues notes in Guitar 2 while MP3 track 65 is playing.

3. Ask the class to perform each guitar part with the recording.

   a. Divide the class into three sections. Assign each section a guitar part in unison using the CD as accompaniment. Use the SI Player to slow the tempo down.

   b. Once students are comfortable with a part have them shift to a different part.

   c. Circulate throughout, helping as needed.

   d. Ask the class to switch parts, and repeat the above process.

OBSERVATIONAL ASSESSMENTS

- Students are counting and playing the melody and counter melody with the correct swing feel.
- Chords are changing on the correct beat and the long–short staccato accents are observed, providing more drive to the rhythm guitar part.
- Students are listening and trying to blend the parts into a whole.
- Students are following the accidentals carefully and using the indicated picking.

INNOVATIONS @HOME

Ask students to research traditional jazz, jazz guitarists, or Charlie Christian online. Find recorded versions of early jazz guitar pieces, both solo and in jazz groups. There are many great historic jazz guitar performances on YouTube.

SOUND ADVICE

"Charlie Christian ...That cat tore everybody's head up."

— WES MONTGOMERY

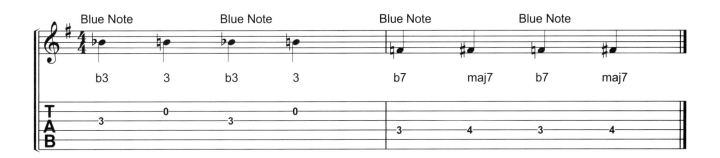

LESSON 5 | Looking Back

GOALS
- Students will review and perform selected pieces of music.
- Students will assist each other and work together in performing ensembles.
- Students will review music theory.

NATIONAL STANDARDS NS1 (Singing), NS2 (Playing), NS5 (Reading), NS6 (Listening), NS7 (Evaluating), NS8 (Making Connections), NS9 (History & Culture)

LESSON 5A (Technique Review)

1. Use line 51, "Chromatic Strength Builder," on page 24 of the student book as a warm-up.

  a. Review the sharps and flats and discuss their location on the guitar neck (sharp is up a fret and flat is down a fret from the natural note).

b. Students should be using all four left hand fingers— one finger per fret.

c. The following is a great technique and right/left hand coordination study. Instruct students to play the same chromatic pattern, but to play each note twice, as shown below.

LESSON 5B (Repertoire Review)

The students have studied numerous performance quality duets and ensembles. The chords and patterns used in these pieces will continue to be used by the students in all future guitar endeavors. Mastery comes with repetition and time, so it is important to review. What follows is a list of key pieces studied to date. Break the students into groups of two or three and have them select one (or more) songs from the list below to review. There is a range of difficulty here, however, playing difficult material is not the issue or goal. The end goal and assessment criteria for whichever song each group selects should be musicality and quality of performance, not difficulty. Songs to choose from:

Page 22: "Flamenco Mood"
Page 23: "Ode to Joy"
Page 26: "One-Grip Blues"
Page 30: "Simple Gifts"
Page 32: "Für Elise"

SOUND SUGGESTIONS

A group leader should be assigned for each ensemble. Encourage students to give each other feedback and suggestions as to how to improve their performances.

LESSON 5C (Review Music Theory, Page 29)

1. Review the C major scale

  a. Ask the class to sing the scale using solfege syllables: do–re–mi–fa–sol–la–ti–do

  b. Try other starting pitches and sing the major scale from each one. Discuss that the major scale is always relative, or the same. Regardless of the names of the pitches, the basic major scale sound (do–re–me …) remains.

  c. Next repeat the process using numbers instead of pitches: 1–2–3–4–5–6–7–8. So all we are doing is substituting numbers for the solfege syllables.

  d. Try this from various pitches. Again, point out how each scale is relatively the same. Note to the class how the scale resolves on "8."

  e. Write several major scales on the white board. Ask the class to count up from the first note in each scale and indentify the I and the V for each.

LESSON 5D (Review Playing by Ear, Page 29)

Pick a song from the list of two chord songs below and distribute the lyric sheet (worksheet #s 17–24) to the class (available at www.alfred.com/SoundInnovations/SIGuitar).

Each of these songs use just two chords: the I chord (C) and the V7 chord (G7). The starting chord is provided above the lyrics. Together, the class will identify all the rest of the chord changes and mark each one above the correct syllable on their handouts. There are several methods for this. Refer back to Level 4/Lesson 1C for the process.

"Down in the Valley"
"My Darlin' Clementine"
"Farmer in the Dell"
"Mary Had a Little Lamb"
"Merrily We Roll Along"
"Polly Wolly Doodle"
"Shoo Fly, Don't Bother Me"
"Three Blind Mice"

SOUND ADVICE

This is a perfect time to introduce the capo. Students can purchase one at any local music store. Using a capo allows guitarists to change the sounding pitch and key of chords without learning new chord forms. For example, placing a capo at the 1st fret and playing the C–G7 chords will sound as C#–G#7. At the 2nd fret it will be D–A7, and so on. Experiment to find comfortable singing keys for each student.

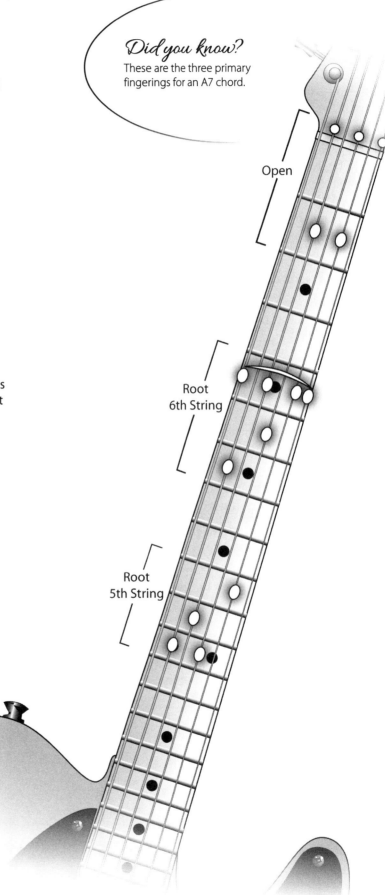

Did you know?
These are the three primary fingerings for an A7 chord.

Open

Root
6th String

Root
5th String

LESSON 6 | Review and Assessment

GOALS
- Review key songs.
- Perform etudes and ensembles that include accented notes, tied notes, pick up measures, and chromatic runs.
- Solidify single-string notes and chords learned to date, including C, G, D, E, Em, Am, A7, D7, and E7.
- Alternate picking with a swing feel, fingerpicking, and accented staccato strum patterns.
- Assess student progress and determine individual needs and goals for progress.

NATIONAL STANDARDS NS1 (Singing), NS2 (Playing), NS5 (Reading), NS6 (Listening), NS7 (Evaluating), NS8 (Making Connections), NS9 (History & Culture)

LESSON 6A: CHORDS, MUSIC THEORY, AND PLAYING BY EAR (Pages 28 and 29)

1. Review and assess Level 4/Lesson 1A.

   a. Ask the class to discuss the information at the top of page 28 of the student book.

   b. Play the different chord qualities on your guitar or at the piano and ask the class to identify whether each chord is major, minor, or dominant seventh.

   c. Do students understand the music theory behind indentifying the I and V chords from a scale?

   d. Can the class apply this theory to the key of G?

2. Play DVD chapter 28 to review the C to G7 chord change.

   a. Can the students execute this chord change in tempo?

   b. Can the class perform both guitar parts for line 57 in tempo with a steady beat?

3. Review and assess "He's Got the Whole World in His Hands" (page 29 of the student book).

   a. Can the students identify the appropriate time for the chord changes?

   b. Can the students create an appropriate strum or fingerpicking pattern for this song without losing the beat? Tell the students not to worry if they can't tell when to change chords. This is a skill that takes time and experience to develop.

   c. Can the students use this technique with other two-chord songs from the list at the bottom of page 29?

LESSON 6B: SIMPLE GIFTS (Pages 30 and 31)

1. Review "Musical Road Maps" at the top of page 30 of the student book.

   a. Ask class to discuss the terms *Coda* (⊕), *D.S. al Coda*, and *To Coda*.

   b. Play MP3 track 61 and have the students follow along with the music.

2. Review and assess "Simple Gifts."

   a. Can students accurately play the melody? Are they executing the pickup notes properly?

   b. Ask half the class to play the melody and ask the other half to play the accompaniment.

   c. Who needs assistance with the pattern and who needs help with making the chord changes?

   d. Is there a nice blend between guitar parts? Are there dynamics?

   e. Are students able to play and sing at a medium tempo?

LESSON 6C: FÜR ELISE (Pages 32 and 33)

1. Review and assess "Für Elise."

   a. Guitar 1: Do students use the correct right hand technique with alternate picking for the eighth notes? Can the students successfully read the accidentals in the music?

   b. Guitar 2: Are students able to count and feel the quarter note pulse with the right hand strum? Can the students apply the optional "Fingerpicking Pattern No. 2" to the ensemble?

   c. Can the students successfully navigate tempo directions such as the fermata and "a tempo"?

LESSON 6D: WHEN THE SAINTS GO MARCHIN' IN (Pages 34 and 35)

1. Review and assess Guitar 3: the chords C, G, G7, D, and D7; playing staccato; and playing accented staccato.

   a. Can the students switch chords with the fingers moving as a unit?

   b. Can the students maintain the indicated strum style with all of the chord changes?

2. Review and assess Guitar 1 and Guitar 2.

   a. Can students correctly play the melody and counter melody with the swing feel?

   b. Identify who needs assistance with the melody or counter melody.

   c. Are students able to play the blue notes in the counter melody?

   d. Is there a nice blend between guitar parts?

   e. Ask the students to switch parts. How well do they perform the new part?

   f. Mark observations in your grade book.

LESSON 6E: FORMAL ASSESSMENTS FOR LEVEL 4

1. Students will form into groups/ensembles with one person on a part. Each ensemble will select one of the following pieces to perform for the class. The students will pick a name for their ensemble and announce it to the class before performing their selection. There are significant differences in difficulty between the songs, however, the critical element is how musically the students perform and present their selected song. At this point their ensemble repertoire is growing and it may be time to think about a brief concert for other classes, parents, or at a school assembly.

   a. "Simple Gifts" (pages 30 and 31)

   b. "Für Elise" (pages 32 and 33)

   c. "When the Saints Go Marchin' In" (pages 34 and 35)

2. Review with students the scoring and assessment criteria for recording their progress. You can use Worksheet #25 to grade performances, and distribute Worksheet #25a so students can create peer evaluations.

   a. Chords are clear, all notes ring clearly without any muffled or muted strings.

   b. Pick is held between the thumb and 1st finger.

   c. Fingerpicking patterns use the correct right-hand approach.

3. As the students perform, look at and observe their musical skills:

   a. Accuracy in the rhythms.

   b. Are the students able to find the correct places to change chords? The more they listen to the relationship between the melody and the correct chord, the more quickly and easily their ears will develop.

   c. Notes and chords are correct.

   d. Performances have a steady tempo.

   e. Appropriate musicality is presented, such as dynamics and accents. Attention should also be paid to performance and form indications such as fermata, "a tempo," 𝄋, *D.S.*, *Coda* (⊕), and *D.S. al Coda*.

SOUND ADVICE

Discuss that all music is actually played by ear, even if you're reading music or playing something someone has shown you. Musicians should always try to hear the piece in their head. Students should try this without playing the guitar and then strive to play like what's imagined in their inner hearing.

LESSON 1 | Three-Chord Rock and Roll

 GOALS
- Students will perform a classic rock and roll rhythm guitar pattern that they can employ in many songs.
- Students will learn about key signatures.
- Students will learn to identify the I, IV, and V chords of a key.

 NATIONAL STANDARDS NS2 (Playing), NS3 (Improvising), NS5 (Reading), NS6 (Listening), NS9 (History & Culture)

LESSON 1A
(Three-Chord Rock and Roll, Page 36)

1. The term "three-chord rock and roll" is commonly used to describe many basic rock songs built on the I, IV, and V chords. It is not used to describe blues, which is its own classification using the same three chords but in a specific 12-bar form and style. Many songs described as "three-chord rock and roll" follow similar if not the exact same chord sequences and rhythm patterns. One of the most common three-chord rock and roll chord patterns is shown on page 36 of the student book. This exact chord sequence can be found in countless songs including "Wild Thing," "Hang on Sloopy," "Twist and Shout," "Louie, Louie," "La Bamba," "Get Off of My Cloud," "Good Lovin'," "Love Is All Around," "You've Lost that Lovin' Feelin'," and many more.

   Note *When learning guitar, it's important to understand that all songs have many things in common. So as you learn a chord progression or a standard rhythm pattern for a song, you are actually learning something that can be applied, and that you will play again, on many, many other songs.*

2. Play DVD chapter 32 or MP3 track 66 for the class. It is very important that students are familiar with the sound and rhythm of lines 66–68 before they attempt to play them.

   a. Line 66: "Three-Chord Rock and Roll in G." Students already know these three chords. What they need to learn here is the rhythm and being able to change chords fast enough to play the pattern.

   b. Using the SI Player slow the track down so students can play along.

   c. "Wild Thing" and "Louie, Louie" are medium slow tempo songs that use this progression. Students can sing the lyrics to those while playing the chord progression.

LESSON 1B
(More Three-Chord Rock and Roll, Page 36)

1. Write out a G major scale on the white board.

   a. Ask the class to sing the scale using solfege syllables: do–re–mi–fa–sol–la–ti–do

   b. Next repeat the process using numbers instead of pitches (1–2–3–4–5–6–7–8). So all we are doing is substituting numbers for the solfege syllables.

   c. Ask the class to identify the I, IV, and V chords in the key of G. These are the three chords they played in line 66.

2. Write out the A major and D major scales on the white board.

   A major: A–B–C♯–D–E–F♯–G♯–A

   D major: D–E–F♯–G–A–B–C♯–D

   a. Ask the class to identify the I, IV, and V chords in each key (A, D, and E7; and D, G, and A7, respectively).

   b. Line 67, "Three-Chord Rock and Roll in D." Students already know these three chords. They will now apply the basic rhythm pattern as heard on MP3 track 67.

   c. Using the SI Player slow the track down so students can play along.

   d. Experiment with singing the previously mentioned songs over this progression.

   e. Finally, do the same with line 68 in the key of A.

SOUND ADVICE

Locate examples of this type of song on YouTube. Some suggested searches:

"Good Lovin'" (The Young Rascals)
"Hang on Sloopy" (The McCoys)
"La Bamba" (Buddy Holly)
"Louie, Louie" (The Kingsmen)
"Twist and Shout" (The Beatles)

LESSON 1C
(Review Playing by Ear, Page 29)

1. Play DVD chapter 28 for the class.

2. Distribute Worksheet #16. These are the lyrics for "He's Got the Whole World in His Hands."

3. This song uses just two chords: the I chord (C) and the V7 chord (G7). The starting chord (C) is provided above the lyrics. Together, the class will identify all the rest of the chord changes and mark each one above the correct syllable on their handouts. There are several methods for doing this:

   a. You can begin on the C chord and sing aloud. Do not change chords—ask the class to raise their hands when it sounds bad. Do this several times until they indentify the exact word or syllable where the chord begins to clash—that is where the chord should change to G7. Continue this process throughout the song, remembering that the correct chord will always be either C or G7. Write the chord symbols above the words.

   b. Alternatively, you could listen to the song with guitar accompaniment on the CD, then play along with the minus guitar version (track 60), asking the students to identify when to change chords.

   c. Students can also work individually, strumming and singing the song softly and identifying on the worksheet when to change chords.

SOUND ADVICE

This is not a competition and it will be a very foreign skill to the class. However, it can be a lot of fun and very exciting. It is critical for no one to think they can't do it just because they didn't get it right away. Keep it fun. Laugh off the mistakes—they will happen. It is important to encourage the students to begin listening in this very subjective manner and for them to realize that because the chord progressions to all songs are *so* repetitious and similar, over time, and with practice, they will be able to identify these types of things pretty easily by ear—especially the extremely common progressions like I–V–I, I–IV–V, I–vi–IV–V, etc.

OBSERVATIONAL ASSESSMENTS

• Can students easily relate scale tones (C–D–E–F–G–A–B–C) with their numeric counterparts (1–8)?

• When attempting to decide between the I and the V chord students are listening for the clash between the melody and the current chord.

INNOVATIONS @HOME

Assign a song from the following list of two-chord songs that all begin on the C chord. You can download the free reproducible lyric worksheets (#s 17–24) for each song at www.alfred.com/SoundInnovations/SIGuitar. Ask students to sing the songs at home and use the processes described in class to decide when to change from C to G7.

"Down in the Valley"
"My Darlin' Clementine"
"Farmer in the Dell"
"Mary Had a Little Lamb"
"Merrily We Roll Along"
"Polly Wolly Doodle"
"Shoo Fly, Don't Bother Me"
"Three Blind Mice"

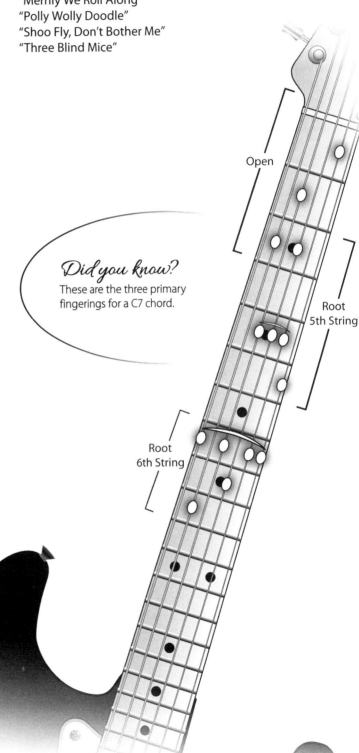

Did you know?
These are the three primary fingerings for a C7 chord.

Open

Root
5th String

Root
6th String

LESSON 2 | Alternating Thumb–Pluck Pattern and Corinna, Corinna

 GOALS
- **Students will learn a new fingerpicking pattern.**
- **Students will perform "Corinna, Corinna," which is American roots music in the country blues vein. This work was first recorded in 1928 by Bo Carter.**
- **Students will follow performance directives.**
- **Students will learn two new guitar chords.**

NATIONAL STANDARDS — **NS1** (Singing), **NS2** (Playing), **NS5** (Reading), **NS6** (Listening), **NS7** (Evaluating), **NS8** (Making Connections)

LESSON 2A
(Alternating Thumb–Pluck Pattern, Page 37)

1. Play DVD chapter 33 or MP3 track 69 for the class. It is very important that students are familiar with the sound and feel of any piece before they attempt to play it.

   a. Line 69: Start by holding the G chord and playing the bass notes with the thumb (*p*). The thumb acts as the bass player alternating from one string to another, and the fingers act as the guitar player working independently.

   b. By isolating the thumb first it will establish the alternating thumb bass approach.

   c. Once this thumb pattern is established, add the fingers (just *i* and *m* in this case) on beats 2 and 4. Usually when fingerpicking, the thumb navigates the 6th, 5th, and 4th strings and the fingers pluck the 3rd, 2nd, and 1st strings.

   d. Once the pattern is established for the G chord in line 69 ask the class to apply the same pattern to a C chord—the thumb will alternate between the 5th and 4th strings. Finally, apply the pattern to a D chord—the thumb will alternate between the 4th and 3rd strings, while the fingers will be on the 2nd and 1st strings.

OBSERVATIONAL ASSESSMENTS

- Can students easily maintain the alternating thumb–pluck pattern? When done properly, this technique provides a very solid rhythm with a slight accent on beats 2 and 4.
- Ask students to play the G chord with this pattern for four measures then switch to the C chord. Watch to make sure the students are planting their fingers before they need to fire them to maintain a solid accompaniment on the beat.

LESSON 2B
(Roots Music and Shuffle, Page 37)

1. "Corinna, Corinna" is a 12-bar country blues song in the AAB form. The term "American roots music," or simply "roots music," used to encompass a wide array of styles including bluegrass, country, gospel, old time music, folk, and blues. Many of these early 20th century forms were adapted to popular music by artists ranging from Leadbelly to Peter, Paul and Mary. In addition, gospel music evolved into rhythm and blues via artists like Ray Charles. "Corinna, Corinna" has been recorded by many artists and adapted by such diverse performers as Blind Lemon Jefferson, Muddy Waters, and Bob Dylan. For a great resource visit the PBS site pbs.org/americanrootsmusic.

2. The term "shuffle" is an indication used in rock and blues to let the performer know that the eighth notes are uneven, exactly like the jazz swing feel. One of the main differences is that the bass player will interpret his role differently for these two styles. In swing the bass player will usually play a constant quarter note walking bass, while for a shuffle he or she will tend to play a simpler line emphasizing the root tones and without walking. Listen to blues recordings—you will find that the shuffle rhythm and similar ones are prevalent in blues.

SOUND ADVICE

"Wes Montgomery played impossible things on the guitar because it was never pointed out to him that they were impossible."

— RONNIE SCOTT, JAZZ SAXOPHONIST

LESSON 2C
(New Chord Prep for Corinna, Corinna)

1. Play DVD chapter 34 for the class. There are two new chords the class will have to practice a new voicing for: the G7 chord, and a special new "slash chord," D/F♯.

An exciting thing about learning the guitar is expanding your chord vocabulary. The new voicing we will be learning for the G7 will allow it to work for the alternating thumb–pluck pattern and has a more

dissonant and interesting sound. It's dissonant because of the way the F and G notes lay in the voicing.

Here are the two new chord voicings for G7 and D/F♯. Review these with the class before proceeding to play "Corinna, Corinna."

Note *In the "slash" method of notating a chord, the letter name to the left of the slash is the name of the triad and the letter name to the right of the slash is the bass note at the bottom of the chord voicing. In this case, the F♯ provides a nice bass movement into the G chord.*

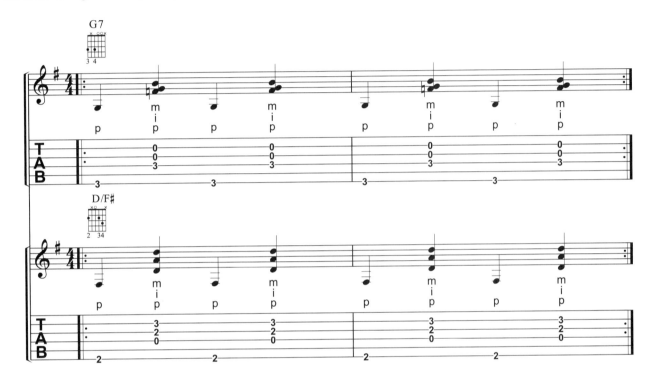

LESSON 2D
(Corinna, Corinna, Page 38)

1. Play DVD chapter 34 or MP3 track 70 for the class. Ask students listen first to the melody and then return to listen to just the accompaniment.

  a. Break the class into two groups. Group 1 will rehearse the melody and Group 2 will rehearse the accompaniment. Assist as needed.

  b. Now switch parts. Group 1 is rehearsing the accompaniment and Group 2 the melody.

  c. Finally, break off into small groups and rehearse the ensemble. Circulate assisting as needed.

SOUND ADVICE

*"I always felt rock and roll
was very, very wholesome music."*
—ARETHA FRANKLIN

Discuss that guitar is not a competition but a creative learning experience, and that guitar concepts may either be familiar or unfamiliar to the class. No matter how familiar or unfamiliar the material is, it is fun and a skill that will help the students to:

- Develop critical thinking by making connections and identifying the main ideas presented.
- Develop the ear.
- Respond to guitar concepts via verbal discussion.
- Reflect on the process of learning to play an instrument, and all manner of additional materials and skills needed to improve and develop into a guitarist and also musician.

INNOVATIONS @HOME

Have the students visit YouTube to find examples of famous guitarists that use the alternating thumb pattern, often called "Travis picking." Famous guitarists known for using this technique include Merle Travis, Chet Atkins, and Doyle Dykes.

LESSON 3 | A Blues Shuffle, Improvised Rhythm Guitar

 GOALS
- Students will learn and perform a foundational rock-blues riff pattern.
- Students will review the 12-bar blues form.
- Students will improvise a guitar strum pattern.
- Students will learn two core guitar chords: A7 and D7.

NATIONAL STANDARDS NS2 (Playing), NS3 (Improvising), NS5 (Reading), NS6 (Listening), NS7 (Evaluating)

LESSON 3A (Introducing the A Blues Shuffle, Page 39)

1. Ask the class to view DVD chapter 35 or MP3 track 72. Students must have the sound of the song in their heads before attempting to play. It gives them a model to emulate and a clear goal for performance.

   a. This is a bass line-style riff played in 2nd position. Have the students follow the left-hand fingerings carefully and use the shuffle rhythm (uneven eighth notes).

   b. Begin with just the pattern for the A7 chord: bar 1. Students should be in 2nd position, use all down-strokes, be aware of the C to C♯ transition, and that F is sharp in the key signature.

   c. Once students are comfortable playing the riff repeatedly with no errors they can apply it to the D7 chord. Just have them take the entire pattern and literally move it to the next string set, the 4th and 3rd strings. Everything stays the same, but it's played on different strings.

   d. Finally, have them move the pattern to the E7 chord—again, everything stays the same, but it's played on the lowest two strings, the 6th and the 5th.

   e. This riff is played with a pick. All down-strokes are preferred.

LESSON 3B (More on the A Blues Shuffle, Page 39)

1. Ask the class to play along with MP3 track 72. You can slow down the playback tempo using the speed control in the SI Player.

2. Discuss the 12-bar blues form. Ask the class to listen and identify the chord changes in terms of the I, IV, and V. They have heard this progression so many times in their lives that they will find it very familiar and their ears will expect each change as it happens.

3. Optional: Ask students to improvise a rhythm guitar part by strumming the indicated chords. This strum pattern should rhythmically complement the bass line pattern.

LESSON 3C (Ensemble Practice on the A Blues Shuffle, Page 39)

1. Break the class into groups. Each group will have a group leader and each person in the group should be assigned one of the guitar parts described below. Circulate throughout the room assisting as needed.

   a. Guitar 1: One guitar plays the part as notated.

   b. Guitar 2: This guitar plays an improvised strum pattern based on the chord diagrams.

   c. Optional Guitar 3: If you have any advanced students who can improvise blues solos they can improvise over the top of the two other parts.

OBSERVATIONAL ASSESSMENTS

- Students are counting and playing the riff with correct timing.
- Students are using all down-strokes.
- Students are changing patterns at the correct time.
- Students are listening and trying to blend the parts into a whole.
- Students are following the accidentals carefully.

LESSON 4 | F Chord, Barre Chords, and Barre Chords by the Bay

GOALS
- •Students will learn the F chord.
- • Students will learn about moveable barre chords.
- • Students will perform "Barre Chords by the Bay."

NATIONAL STANDARDS NS2 (Playing), NS4 (Composing), NS5 (Reading), NS6 (Listening), NS7 (Evaluating), NS8 (Making Connections), NS9 (History & Culture)

LESSON 4A (Playing a Barre F Chord, Page 40)

1. There are certain key principles for the developing guitarist. The concept and execution of moveable "barre" chord forms is one of the main ones. "Barre" simply means that to form the chord, one finger lays across multiple strings. When a chord contains only fretted notes and no open strings it can be moved up and down the neck to create many more chords with the same quality, but different roots (since all notes in the chord move equally, fret-by-fret). The F chord we're introducing here uses a small barre.

2. View DVD chapter 36 for an explanation, and more important, a visual demonstration of how to execute the F barre chord.

3. Technique Tip: Collapse the tip joint of the 1st finger. This will flatten it and effectively cover the two strings that need to be barred at the same time. If the students roll the 1st finger back a bit so more of the bony part is fretting the notes, that can help to clear the 2nd and 1st strings in the F chord. If students have an electric guitar, have them try playing barre chords on it—it is a bit easier than playing them on an acoustic instrument. Also, it is much easier to play barre chords higher up the neck where there is significantly less string tension. Once the F chord shape is learned have the class move it up the neck and practice obtaining a clear sound in higher positions.

4. Keep in mind that it is possible to change the strings on an acoustic instrument to light or extra light. This will make playing barre chords easier but may decrease the volume and projection of the instrument.

5. Another Tip: Have students play the barre chord at the 7th fret or higher, then slide it down towards the 1st position.

6. There is no magic wand that dispenses easy barring. Students will need to work at it and play each note in the chord to make sure the chord is clear.

LESSON 4B (F Barre Chord Etude, Page 40)

1. First practice finding the location for each of the chords in the etude using the root tone on the 1st string.

   a. Remember that any chord with an accidental is only a half step below the guide chord (♭) or a half step above the guide chord (♯).

   b. Play along with MP3 track 74.

- • Students are changing to the correct root and chord on the correct beat.
- • Students are not losing the shape of the chord as it is moved to play from the appropriate root.
- • Students are following the accidentals carefully.

LESSON 4C (Barre Chords by the Bay, Page 40)

1. It is amazing how the guitar opens up once the moveable barre technique is available to the student. This song is in the style of the late great Otis Redding's "Dock of the Bay." It is a good idea to listen to the original song (on YouTube or elsewhere) and get the feel of the syncopation—especially note the tie from measure 1 to 2. Use the SI Player to slow down the track and find a tempo that makes it easy for your students play and master the song.

- • Chords are changing on the correct beat.
- • Students are using syncopation in their rhythm strums.
- • Students are following the accidentals carefully.

SOUND ADVICE

"Otis was one of those kind of guys who had 100 ideas. Anytime he came in to record he always had 10 or 15 different intros or titles, or whatever. He had been at San Francisco playing The Fillmore, and he was staying at a boathouse, which is where he got the idea of the ship coming in. That's about all he had: 'I watch the ships come in and I watch them roll away again.'"

— GUITARIST STEVE CROPPER

INNOVATIONS @HOME

Ask students to research Otis Redding and his song "Dock of the Bay" online. Find recorded versions of the original piece and locate arrangements and performances by other artists.

LESSON 5 | Looking Back

GOALS
- Students will review and perform selected pieces of music.
- Students will assist each other and work together in performing ensembles.
- Students will review music theory.

NATIONAL STANDARDS NS1 (Singing), NS2 (Playing), NS3 (Improvising), NS5 (Reading), NS6 (Listening), NS7 (Evaluating), NS8 (Making Connections), NS9 (History & Culture)

LESSON 5A
(Three-Chord Rock and Roll Review, Page 36)

1. Write out a G major scale on the white board.

2. Ask the class to sing the scale using solfege syllables (do–re–me …) then numbers (1–2–3 …).

3. Now ask the class to identify the I, IV, and V chords in the key of G. Write out other major scales on the board and ask the class to identify the I, IV, and V chords in each.

4. Lines 66–68: Using the SI Player, slow the tracks down so students can play along. Ask the class to perform all three lines.

5. Are students are playing the correct rhythm and changing chords on the correct beats? If not, this can be a long-term goal for these patterns.

LESSON 5B
(Corinna, Corinna Review, Pages 37 and 38)

1. Play DVD chapter 34 for the class.

2. Review the basic thumb–pluck pattern for the G and D/F♯ chords.

3. Ask the class to break into groups and select a leader for each. Each member of each group should be assigned to either Guitar 1 (melody), Guitar 2 (thumb–pluck pattern), or an optional Guitar 3 (an improvised strum pattern based on the indicated guitar chords).

4. Students should rehearse the song. Circulate throughout assisting as needed.

5. Are students counting and playing the thumb–pluck pattern with a solid time feel?

6. Are students using the alternating thumb consistently?

7. Are students listening and trying to blend the parts into a whole?

8. Are students successfully playing the new chord forms for G7 and D/F♯?

LESSON 5C (A Blues Shuffle Review, Page 39)

1. Review the 12-bar blues form.

2. Break the class in groups. Each group will have a group leader and each person in the group should be assigned one of the guitar parts described below. Circulate throughout the room assisting as needed.

   a. Guitar 1: One guitar plays the part as notated.

   b. Guitar 2: This guitar plays an improvised strum pattern based on the chord diagrams.

   c. Optional Guitar 3: If you have any advanced students who can improvise blues solos they can improvise over the top of the two other parts.

3. Are students counting and playing the riff with correct timing?

4. Are students using all down-strokes?

5. Are students changing patterns at the correct time?

6. Are students listening and trying to blend the parts into a whole?

7. Are students following the accidentals carefully?

LESSON 5D
(Barre Chords by the Bay Review, Page 40)

1. Play MP3 track 75. As an option also play the original version of Otis Redding's "Dock of the Bay."

2. Review the concept of movable barre chords: Any chord fingering with no open strings can be moved to different frets, transposing the chord up or down in half steps, fret by fret.

3. Ask the class to perform "Barre Chords by the Bay" and assist as needed.

4. Are students moving the chord form to the correct frets?

5. Are students making the changes and not losing the shape of the major chord as it is moved to play the appropriate root and chord?

6. Are students following the rhythm and successfully playing the chromatic chord sequence in bar 3?

LESSON 6 | Review and Assessment

GOALS
- **Review key songs.**
- **Perform ensembles that build a solid repertoire for concerts.**
- **Assess and determine individual needs and goals.**

NATIONAL STANDARDS
NS2 (Playing), **NS3** (Improvising), **NS5** (Reading), **NS6** (Listening), **NS7** (Evaluating), **NS8** (Making Connections), **NS9** (History & Culture)

LESSON 6A: FORMAL ASSESSMENTS FOR LEVEL 5

1. Students will form into groups/ensembles with one person on a part. Each ensemble will select one of the following pieces to perform for the class.

a. "Three Chord Rock and Roll" (in G, D, or A, page 36)

b. "Corinna, Corinna" using the alternating thumb–pluck pattern (page 38)

c. "A Blues Shuffle" (page 39)

d. "Barre Chords by the Bay" (page 40)

2. Set up a performance area for the class. Place the chairs, method books, and stands at the front of the class. Each ensemble needs to be organized beforehand and come up with a name for the group. Tuning should be checked off stage and students should line up for a walk to the stage to present their performance.

a. When the students walk up to perform, the class should acknowledge them with applause.

b. The performers should acknowledge the audience with a bow.

c. One person in the ensemble will announce the piece and any researched historical or pertinent information for the work. Usually this person will start the count-off.

d. At the end of the performance the ensemble will stand together and take a bow together.

e. The group leader will initiate standing and bowing and the ensemble should walk off the stage together.

3. Use Worksheet #26 to assess the following, and distribute Worksheet #26a so that students can create peer assessments:

a. Technique

   i. Chords are clear, all notes ring without any muffled or muted strings.

   ii. Barred notes are played appropriately and have a clear, focused sound.

   iii. Pick is held between the thumb and 1st finger.

   iv. Fingerpicking patterns use the correct right hand approach.

b. Musical skills

   i. Accuracy in the rhythms.

   ii. Notes and chords are correct.

   iii. Performances have a steady tempo.

c. Form and performance indications

   i. Dynamics

   ii. Accents

   iii. Fermata, A tempo

   iv. Repeats, *D.S. al Coda*, and *Coda* (⊕)

4. Ask students to visualize the chord fingerings. Can they picture them? Ask them to close their eyes for a second and try to picture the shape of a chord form and the way the fingers change from one chord to the next. If they can use visualization for the fingerings and how one chord form changes to another, it will be much easier for them to change chord forms. The more they practice the guitar with visualization, the quicker they will be able to improve.

Did you know?
These are the three primary fingerings for an F chord.

Root
6th String

Root
5th String

Root
5th String

LESSON 1 | Minuet in G

 GOALS
- Students will perform a trio based on "Minuet in G," from Johann Sebastian Bach's *Notebook for Anna Magdalena*.
- Students will perform and discuss melody, harmony, and chord accompaniment.
- Students will use dynamics.

 NATIONAL STANDARDS **NS2** (Playing), **NS5** (Reading), **NS6** (Listening), **NS7** (Evaluating), **NS8** (Making Connections), **NS9** (History & Culture)

LESSON 1A (Minuet in G, Page 41)

1. Play DVD chapter 37 or MP3 track 76 for the class and review the basics of the piece:

a. It's in $\frac{3}{4}$

b. Guitar 1 is melody; Guitar 2 fills out the song, adds rhythmic drive, and harmonizes with the melody; and Guitar 3 is the strumming accompaniment.

c. Review the dynamic markings and point them out throughout the arrangement.

2. Break the class into three groups, each assigned to one part. Each group should have a group leader. Circulate throughout the room, helping as needed and elaborating on the following:

a. Guitar 1 is the melody. Students should be especially wary of the key signature—the song is in the key of G, so all Fs are sharp. Point out the F♯ notes in bars 3, 7, and 9.

b. Guitar 2: This is an interesting eighth note rhythm. This entire part constantly alternates between just the 3rd and 4th strings. This is basically an arpeggio-style part—students can hold the chord forms and play the strings, letting all notes ring. Point out that holding a chord and working out an arpeggio pattern on just two or three strings this is a good way to build a part. We're suggesting strict alternate picking for this, but all down-strokes can work also.

c. Guitar 3: A simple strum pattern based on just G, C, and D7—even Bach played three-chord music. Students can experiment with adding some eighth note strums once the rhythm is solid. Also, some students can strum while others apply the $\frac{3}{4}$ fingerpicking pattern to the chords.

LESSONS 1B AND 1C

Now switch up the parts and proceed as just outlined. All students should have the opportunity to perform all three parts.

SOUND ADVICE

"To play the guitar well is easy;
to play the guitar poorly is difficult."

— PEPE ROMERO

Ask students to find versions of "Minuet in G" on YouTube. They should also check out "A Lover's Concerto," a top 10 hit for The Toys in 1965 that is based on "Minuet in G."

SOUND EXPECTATIONS

Guitar 1 will not be hard once the students have the melody in their ears. Guitar 2 is easy once the class understands that it is simply a two-note alternating arpeggio pattern based on the G, C, and D chords. Guitar 3 should also be pretty playable, in tempo. Encourage students to improvise variations on the simple quarter-note strum pattern.

OBSERVATIONAL ASSESSMENTS

- Are students able to perform together as an ensemble, with good timing and interaction related to dynamics, tempos, etc.?
- Students should have the chords memorized and should be able to play fingerpicking patterns from memory without having to refer to tablature or music.

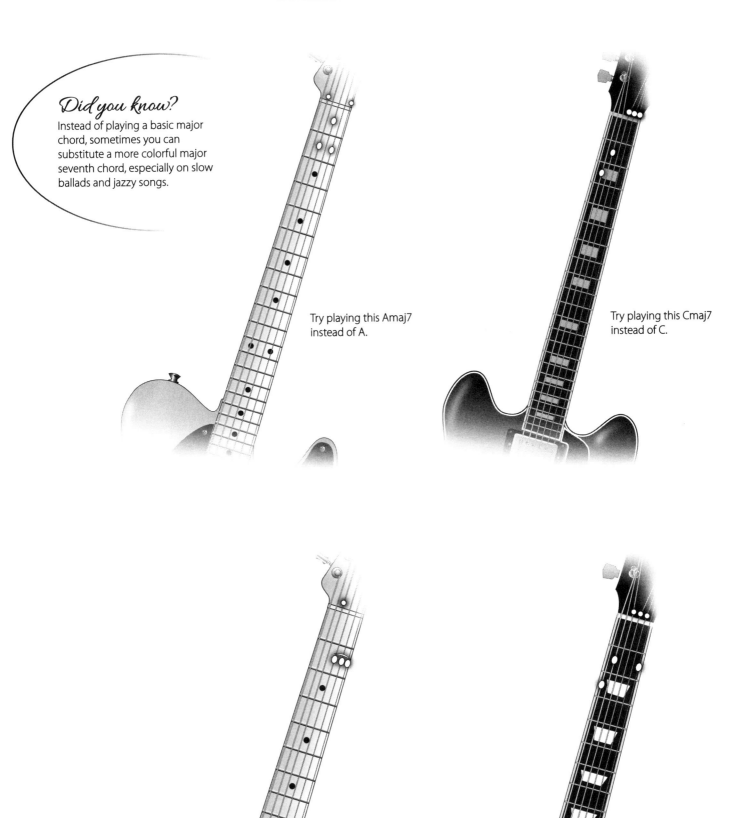

Did you know?
Instead of playing a basic major chord, sometimes you can substitute a more colorful major seventh chord, especially on slow ballads and jazzy songs.

Try playing this Amaj7 instead of A.

Try playing this Cmaj7 instead of C.

Try playing this Dmaj7 instead of D.

Try playing this Gmaj7 instead of G.

LESSON 2 | Aguado Study, plus Dm

GOALS
- Students count, play, and read melody in the lower register of the guitar; play fingerstyle; and strum accompaniments.
- Students will use the 3rd position.
- Perform an ensemble work derived from a traditional classical guitar repertoire piece with appropriate dynamics.
- Research 19th century guitar studies such as the work of Dionisio Aguado and Fernando Sor.
- Students will compare and contrast alternate and glide picking.
- Students will learn a new chord, Dm, and a new chord change, A7–Dm.

NATIONAL STANDARDS NS2 (Playing), NS5 (Reading), NS6 (Listening), NS7 (Evaluating), NS8 (Making Connections), NS9 (History & Culture)

LESSON 2A (New Chord: Dm, Page 42)

1. Play DVD chapter 38 or MP3 track 78 for the class. Review the basics of the piece.

2. Have the students study the diagram for the new chord they will be learning: Dm. Draw the chord diagram for D major on the board and be sure to include the fingerings.

3. Ask the students to identify which notes are different between D and Dm.

   a. Instruct the class as to the theory behind major and minor chords. Draw a line of notes on the board from D to A in the key of D—D, E, F♯, G, and A. The D major chord uses the notes D, F♯, and A. Since in a minor chord the 3rd is lowered by a half step, to get D minor one would play the notes D, F natural, and A.

   b. Since we'd have to lower the note on the 1st string in the D major chord a half step to make it minor, we can see from the diagram that the F natural in the D minor chord makes perfect sense. A minor chord contains the root, the lowered 3rd, and the 5th.

4. Next have students identify the movements required when playing the A7–Dm chord change.

   a. Have the students follow the directions at the top of page 42 of the student book and listen to MP3 track 77. When changing from A7 to Dm, the 2nd finger should be used as a guide—it that stays in the same spot on the neck but moves down one string (towards the floor), while the 3rd finger slides up a fret and the 1st finger is added. When going from Dm to A7, the process is reversed—the 2nd finger moves up one string (towards the ceiling), while the 3rd finger slides down a fret and the 1st finger is lifted off the fretboard.

   b. Ask the class to practice moving from the A7 to Dm chords. Also have them write each chord diagram five times in their manuscript paper, then simply visualize the chords.

LESSON 2B (Prepare to Perform the Aguado Study, Page 42)

1. Play DVD chapter 38 or MP3 track 78 for the class. They should follow along with the score on page 42.

2. Instruct the students to play a D and Dm. Note that the 3rd finger stays in the same spot, and that to change one note the students may have to move more than one finger.

3. Pay close attention to the DVD's explanation and demonstration of measures 3 and 11, in which the 3rd position is used to facilitate a smooth articulation of the accompaniment.

   a. It is important that you have an aim in mind and use a concept by the great guitar pedagogue Aaron Shearer: "Aim Directed Movement," or the acronym ADM. This concept is simple: you see in your mind's eye the finger shape and its position, and then fingers immediately follow through. When practicing a work with the ADM principle, you can eliminate mistakes and speed the process of memorizing and performing a piece of music. Start slow, find a tempo at which you can use ADM, and play the passage accurately.

   b. Isolate these measures to get the technique under the students' fingers. Ask the class to repeatedly play measures 3 and 4 to get used to moving between the 1st and 3rd positions.

   c. The notes should ring out. By using the suggested fingerings, the chord changes can be easily navigated.

   d. Once the right hand fingering and 3rd position left hand fingering are under control, have the students play the passage beginning on measure 2 and ending on measure 5.

   e. Have the students rehearse each individual measure before they play the entire piece.

LESSON 2C (Perform the Aguado Study, Page 42)

1. Ask students break into their groups for practice.

2. Students should use a medium slow tempo to rehearse the song. Ask the students to assist and provide constructive feedback to each other.

3. Ask one student in each group to add the optional Guitar 3 part.

> Note *Have students try the sequence with glide picking and compare it to alternate picking. With glide picking (also known as sweep picking), a guitarist may play several consecutive down- or up-strokes in a row, "gliding" the pick through the strings. In this case, the picking sequence would be down, down, down, up. Notice that glide picking tends to make it easier to accent the downbeats on 1 and 3.*

SOUND ADVICE

"One must make of one's fingers well-drilled soldiers."

— FERNANDO SOR

Ask students to find information from the early guitar methods by Aguado and Sor. Have them also find background information on Aguado's life. What was going on in other areas of music, and history in general, in their time?

SOUND EXPECTATIONS

Students performing Guitar 1 should be able to maintain the *p–i–m–i* fingerpicking pattern and find a tempo where the pulse of the song is even. Students performing Guitar 2 should be able to play the melody and bring it out so it is balanced with guitars 1 and 2. Students performing Guitar 3 should try both the alternate picking strum and the new glide picking strum. Make sure the students are familiar with all three parts and have used the SI Player to practice with MP3 track 78 using the three "minus" options.

OBSERVATIONAL ASSESSMENTS

• Are students able to perform together as an ensemble, with good timing and interaction related to dynamics, tempos, etc.?

• The students are comfortable switching between the 1st and 3rd position for Guitar 1.

• Students have developed their performance skills; they bow, present the titles, and give some background on the pieces they play.

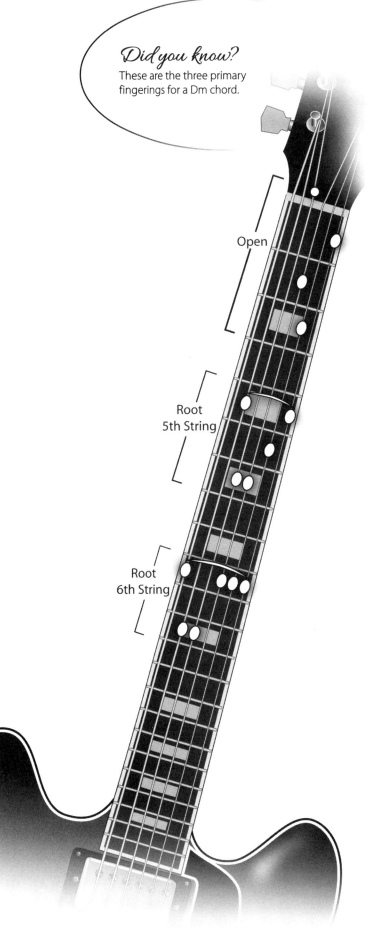

Did you know?
These are the three primary fingerings for a Dm chord.

Open

Root
5th String

Root
6th String

LESSON 3 | Triplets and Blues

 GOALS
- Students will count and play eighth note triplets.
- Students will use triplets in the context of an authentic blues shuffle.
- Students will learn and perform several classic blues rhythm patterns.

NATIONAL STANDARDS **NS2** (Playing), **NS3** (Improvising), **NS5** (Reading), **NS6** (Listening), **NS7** (Evaluating), **NS8** (Making Connections)

LESSON 3A (Triplets, Page 43)

1. Play DVD chapter 39 or MP3 track 79 for the class.

   a. Eighth-note triplets are three eighth notes played in the space of two.

   b. They are counted very evenly: 1–a–let, 2–a–let, 3–a–let, 4–a–let, with the foot tapping on 1, 2, 3, 4.

   c. On pages 34 and 37 of the student book, the class learned about the swing feel and shuffle rhythm, both of which feature uneven eighth notes (long–short). Those uneven eighth notes are actually the same as playing the first and third parts of the triplet.

   > **Note** *In popular music, especially blues and jazz, the underlying feel/subdivision of the quarter note is often in three equal parts, not two. In jazz, this rhythm is called the swing rhythm (also marked by a walking bass line) and in blues it is called the shuffle rhythm (typically with no walking bass). So this means that the feel of the rhythm dictates that each quarter breaks naturally into three equal parts (triplet) or two uneven eighth notes.*

2. Line 79: "Triplet Example No. 1." This demonstrates how to play the triplet rhythm using the one-grip blues pattern" (pages 25–27 of the student book).

   a. Play MP3 track 79, use the SI Player to loop the example, and ask the class to count and clap the rhythm aloud along with the recording.

   b. Once the class is comfortable with the rhythm ask them to play along with the recording.

3. Line 80 is a visual illustration of the rhythmic alignment of triplets to uneven eighths and quarter notes. Review the note alignment with the class and then assign parts and play. The top part is the triplet figure, the middle is a basic blues shuffle bass line (uneven eighth notes), and the bottom part is a basic quarter note pulse.

LESSON 3B (One-Finger Blues Riff, Page 43)

1. Line 81: "One-Finger Blues Riff." This riff is a classic blues rhythm pattern, most associated with T-Bone Walker's "Stormy Monday." Students will first learn the pattern over the A7 chord and then transpose it to work over the D7 and E7 chords before applying it to a 12-bar blues form.

   a. Play MP3 track 81 for the class. You can also show them DVD chapter 40 as a prelude to learning this pattern.

   b. For the A7 riff: This is played with an uneven eighth-note feel. Students play the open A bass notes on "1–and" followed by the chord riff on "2–and." Barre the top three strings at the 2nd fret with the 1st finger. Play the chord then release and play the three open strings. Play repeatedly until a nice blues shuffle feel is achieved.

   c. For the D7 riff: Students play the open D bass notes then barre the top three strings at the 7th fret with the 1st finger. Play the chord then quickly slide the 1st finger barre down two frets to the 5th fret. The slide should be strong enough to sound the 5th fret chord without using the pick again. If students don't have the strength for the slide yet, they can just move down two frets and strike the strings again.

   d. For the E7 riff: Students play the open E bass notes then barre the top three strings at the 9th fret with the 1st finger. Play the chord then slide down to the 7th fret like we did for the D7 riff.

LESSON 3C (One-Finger Blues, Pages 44–45)

1. Play DVD chapter 40 or MP3 track 82 for the class.

2. This song is a shuffle blues combining three classic patterns. Discuss the three parts the class will perform and the key performance goals.

    a. Guitar 1: This is the classic blues rhythm riff based on the "Stormy Monday" pattern that we are calling the "One-Finger Blues Riff." This is the rhythm guitar part.

    b. Guitar 2: This is the "A Blues Shuffle" line that students played on page 39. This is the bass line.

    c. Guitar 3: On the repeat students will play "The One-Grip Blues Pattern" they learned on page 25 of the student book. This is the lead guitar part, also called the guitar solo.

SOUND ADVICE

• All students should have the opportunity to learn and perform all three parts.

• Drop out the Guitar 3 part and instead select individual students to play improvised guitar solos. Students should begin improvising by using the basic one-grip pattern and its variations suggested on page 25.

INNOVATIONS @HOME

Ask students to locate recordings or videos of "Stormy Monday." Many artists have recorded the song. The recording most similar to the riff in this version is by The Allman Brothers Band.

OBSERVATIONAL ASSESSMENTS

• Students are counting and playing with correct timing.

• Students are performing with a nice shuffle feel.

• Chords are changing on the correct beat.

• Students are listening and trying to blend the parts into a whole.

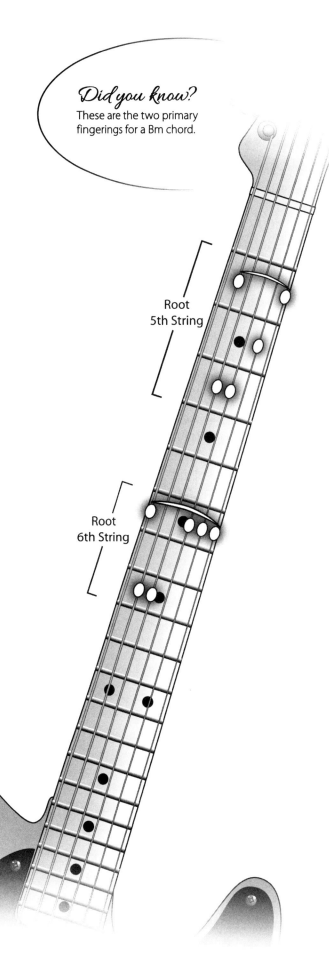

Did you know?
These are the two primary fingerings for a Bm chord.

Root
5th String

Root
6th String

LESSON 4 | Romanza, plus B7, Em9, and Am6

 GOALS

- **Students will perform a trio arrangement of a song that is standard to the classical guitarist's core repertoire.**
- **Students will learn the chords Em9, Am6, and B7.**
- **Students will review music theory.**
- **Students will correctly play the accidentals.**

NATIONAL STANDARDS **NS1** (Singing), **NS2** (Playing), **NS5** (Reading), **NS6** (Listening), **NS7** (Evaluating), **NS8** (Making Connections), **NS9** (History & Culture)

LESSON 4A (New Chords B7, Em9, and Am6, Page 46)

1. Play DVD chapter 41 or MP3 track 83 for the class. Review the basics of the piece, especially the information on the chords, before the ensemble is played.

2. Ask students to review the chord diagrams for the three new chords they will be playing: B7, Em9, and Am6. They're introduced in measures 1, 7, and 11, respectively. Draw the chord diagram for B7 on the board and be sure to include the fingering.

   a. Begin with the B7 chord and go over how it is played, and that the tricky part of this voicing is making sure the open 2nd string (B) is ringing and not muted.

   b. Ask the students to strum the Em9 chord—it has a beautiful modern sound.

      i. Music theory: Write out an E minor scale on the board. Let the students count up from the root note to one note past the octave: E, F♯, G, A, B, C, D, E (octave), and, finally, F♯ (9th). So F♯ is the 9th and it is played with the 4th finger on the 4th string. Adding this note turns Em into Em9.

   c. Once the notes are clear ask the students to practice the fingerpicking patterns. Point out the constant alternation between the thumb and index finger in Guitar 3: *p–i–p–i–p–i–p–i*. Also in this part, the thumb alternates between two strings while the index finger plays the open G string in between each thumb stroke.

   d. The Am6 is played by keeping the 4th finger on the F♯ and moving the 1st to the A on the 3rd string.

   e. Have the class practice alternating between the Em9 and Am6 chords very slowly and increase the speed very slowly until a medium tempo is achieved.

LESSON 4B (Romanza Preparation, Page 46)

1. Play DVD chapter 41 or MP3 track 83 for the class. Again, students should always have the sound of the song in their ears before they attempt to play.

2. Ask students to observe each other playing Guitar 3 to see if they are allowing the repeated notes to ring while playing the complete pattern.

3. Ask the class to break into small groups and select a group leader for each group. Each group will rehearse the song, and all students should have the opportunity to perform all three guitar parts. Circulate throughout assisting as needed.

4. When playing Guitar 1, the melody, students must pay strict attention to the accidentals in the score.

5. When playing Guitar 2, students should maintain the thumbed bass and the repeated block chords in tempo and with a good tone. Practice moving from the Am chord to the B7, Em to B7, and B7 to Em as a preparation for this part.

LESSON 4C (Perform Romanza, Page 46)

1. Ask students to break into their pre-selected groups (trios) for ensemble practice.

2. Students should rehearse the song in a medium slow tempo. Ask the students to assist and provide constructive feedback to each other.

3. Have the groups play each guitar part in unison and then assign one person per part to perform in trios. This is the best time to make the rounds throughout the class.

SOUND ADVICE

"The classical guitar has a dynamic to it unlike a regular acoustic guitar or an electric guitar. You know, there's times when you should play and there's times when you gotta hold back. It's an extremely dynamic instrument."

— STEVE VAI

Ask students to find information on the Spanish folk song "Romanza." Students may also find solo classical guitar performances on YouTube.

SOUND EXPECTATIONS

Guitar 3 will be able to maintain the *p–i–p–i* pattern and find a tempo in which the pulse of the song is even. Guitar 1 can play the melody and bring it out so it is balanced with guitars 2 and 3. Make sure the students are familiar with all three parts and have used the SI Player to practice all three parts.

OBSERVATIONAL ASSESSMENTS

• Are students able to perform together as an ensemble, with good timing and interaction related to dynamics, tempos, etc?

• The students are comfortable switching between the chords, especially the new B7, Em9, and Am6.

• Students are using the correct fingers on the correct strings.

• Accompaniment tones are clear and not muffled.

Did you know?
This is an Am9. Try using it instead of an Am chord, especially for slow songs.

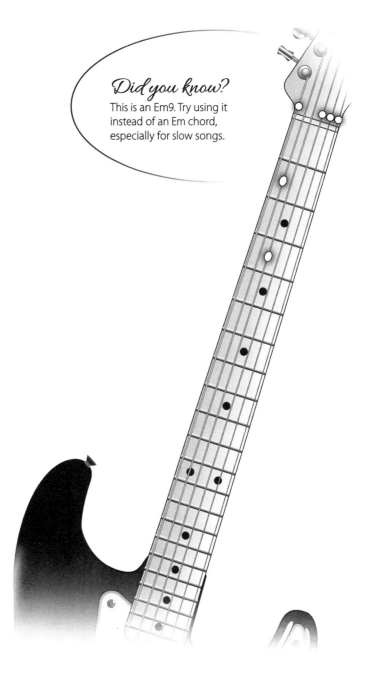

Did you know?
This is an Em9. Try using it instead of an Em chord, especially for slow songs.

LESSON 5 | Simple Gifts

GOALS
- Students will perform a solo guitar arrangement.
- Students will improvise and arrange accompaniment parts.
- Students will review music theory.

NATIONAL STANDARDS NS2 (Playing), NS5 (Reading), NS6 (Listening), NS7 (Evaluating), NS8 (Making Connections), NS9 (History & Culture)

LESSON 5A (Simple Gifts, Page 48)

1. Play DVD chapter 42 for the class, or use MP3 track 84. Again, students should always have the sound of the song in their ears before they attempt to play.

2. Describe to the class that this arrangement is for solo guitar. It is intended to be musically complete on its own with no accompaniment.

   a. In between the melody notes, open strings are used to fill out the sound and support the melody. Let all notes rings as long as possible.

   b. Students should hold down the repeated notes, allowing them to continue to ring while playing the open string filler notes. For example, in measure 2 hold the 3rd fret D note while playing the open G string. In measure 3, hold the 2nd fret A note while playing the open D string.

3. Ask the class to break into small groups, and select a leader for each. Each group will rehearse the song in unison. Circulate throughout assisting as needed.

LESSON 5B (Simple Gifts, Building an Accompaniment, Page 48)

1. Draw a G major scale on the board.

   a. Ask the class to identify the I, IV, and V chords in the key of G (G, C, and D).

   b. Examine the music. What are the chords? Again, this is an example of an entire song that uses only the I, IV, and V chords of the key.

2. Again break into small groups. Each group should have one person performing the arrangement and one or more improvising an accompaniment based on the chord symbols. The accompaniment can be strum-style or based on "Fingerpicking Pattern No. 1."

SOUND ADVICE

Capos can be used to add interest and color when multiple guitars are performing together. Try this:

1. Ask some of the students who are playing the chords (strumming or fingerstyle) to place a capo on the 5th fret—at least half the students playing chords should remain with no capo.

2. With a capo at the 5th fret the guitar has been transposed up a 4th. So that means if students use chord shapes from the key of D, they will sound in concert G, but the voicings will be different and higher than the key of G voicings. It's important to note that when guitarists use a capo, they tend to think in the key of the chord shapes they are playing, not necessarily the concert key. So in this case, the guitarists using a capo at the 5th fret will think of the song in the key of D and use key-of-D chords (D, G, and A) even though those chords will sound in concert G.

3. Review the chords to the song and identify them as I, IV, and V in the key of G.

4. Draw a D major scale on the board and ask the class to identify the I, IV, and V chords (D, G, and A or A7). Now go through the song again and explain that, for those with a capo, the I chord is the D chord shape, the IV chord is the G chord shape, and the V chord is the A chord shape.

5. Ask the students who are playing with a capo to pencil in the key of D chords on the song chart—G becomes D, D becomes A (or A7), and C becomes G.

In essence we are orchestrating the guitars to create a really full sounding ensemble. The key of D chord chart should look like this:

```
/ D        /        / A        /                /
/ D        /        / A        / G    D    /
/ D        /        /          / A           /
/ D        /        / A  D  / G  D  //
```

OBSERVATIONAL ASSESSMENTS

- This is one of the more challenging pieces in this book, especially because the constant flow of eighth notes means students don't have an opportunity to rest or any leeway should they make a mistake. Students should strive for a gentle, but constant, flowing rhythm.

- Is the melody, which is buried within the "filler" notes, coming through? Students need to hear the melody in their head so they will naturally accent those notes.

INNOVATIONS @HOME

"Simple Gifts" is a very popular melody. Ask students to locate recorded versions of this song. There are many great versions available including those by Yo-Yo Ma with Alison Krauss, Jewel, and Aaron Copland's amazing usage of the melody in the piece "Appalachian Spring."

LESSON 6 | Review and Assessment

GOALS
- **Review key songs.**
- **Perform ensembles that build a solid repertoire for concerts.**
- **Develop skill in performance and audience acknowledgement.**
- **Solidify note reading for melodic statements and expand the chord vocabulary to include Dm, B7, Em9, and Am6.**
- **Play a sophisticated blues progression, introduce the class to improvisation, and understand and perform eighth note triplets.**
- **Assess student progress and determine individual needs and goals for final grade.**

NATIONAL STANDARDS NS2 (Playing), NS3 (Improvising), NS5 (Reading), NS6 (Listening), NS7 (Evaluating), NS8 (Making Connections), NS9 (History & Culture)

LESSON 6A: REVIEW AND OBSERVATIONAL ASSESSMENT (Pages 41–48)

1. Review and assess "Minuet in G."

a. Divide the class into three sections and assign a part to each section.

b. Direct each section to practice their part as you scan the room and assist where needed.

c. Have the class perform the ensemble together as a group.

d. If time allows, ask the students to switch parts. Make sure that each student has the opportunity to play all three parts.

2. "Minuet in G," "Aguado Study," "One Finger Blues," "Three-Chord Rock and Roll" (in G, D, and A), "Für Elise," and "Simple Gifts" are all built on just the I, IV, and V chords in their key. Ask the students that given this, why do they sound so drastically different from each other?

LESSON 6B: REVIEW AND OBSERVATIONAL ASSESSMENT (Pages 42–43)

1. Play DVD chapter 38 and MP3 track 78 and have the students follow along with the "Aguado Study" music.

a. Can students follow the musical road map?

b. Can students accurately play the melody?

2. Have a third of the class play the melody, the other third the fingerpicking pattern, and the final third Guitar 3.

a. Who needs assistance with the pattern and who needs help with making the chord changes?

b. Is there a nice blend between guitar parts? Are there dynamics? Can the students explain why the specific dynamics in the score are used?

c. Are students able to play at a medium tempo?

LESSON 6C: REVIEW AND OBSERVATIONAL ASSESSMENT (Pages 43–45)

1. Review and assess all the chords on the bottom of page 43 of the student book.

2. Review and assess "One Finger Blues" on page 44 of the student book.

a. Can students use the correct right hand technique for Guitar 1 with appropriate picking for the eighth notes, all in time? Can the students use ADM (Aim Directed Movement) to place the left hand fingers in the upper areas of the neck?

b. Who needs assistance with the Guitar 2 riff?

c. Are students able to count and feel the quarter note pulse with the right hand?

d. Ask if any of the students would like to improvise a blues solo. This can be as simple as improvising new rhythms using the triplets in Guitar 3. There may be students who have some rock chops, and you can have them improvise while the class plays guitars 1 and 2.

LESSON 6D: REVIEW AND OBSERVATIONAL ASSESSMENT (Pages 46–47)

1. Review and assess "Romanza" on page 46 of the student book.

a. Review the new chords B7, Em9, and Am6.

i. Can the students visualize these chords?

ii. Can the students switch chords with the fingers moving as a unit?

iii. Can the students maintain the fingerpicking *p–i–p–i* with all of the chord changes?

b. Review Guitar 2.

i. Can students correctly play and maintain the thumb–chord pattern? Identify who needs assistance.

ii. Is there a nice blend between guitar parts? Ask the students to switch parts—how well do they perform the new part?

iii. Mark any unusual observations in your grade book.

LESSON 6E: REVIEW AND OBSERVATIONAL ASSESSMENT (Page 48)

1. Review the solo "Simple Gifts."

   a. Can the students maintain alternate picking for the melodic eighth notes?

   b. Can the students switch chords with the fingers moving as a unit?

   c. Are the students keeping the eighth notes even and not swung? Make sure the students are aware that swing eighths may not be appropriate for every song.

2. Review and assess the students' interpretation of "Simple Gifts."

   a. Can students play the chords more softly than the melody?

   b. Is the final chord held for two beats at the end of the song?

   c. The instruction states to play the solo "gently, with feeling." How can the students accomplish this?

      i. During some quiet time, have the students visualize themselves playing "Simple Gifts."

      ii. Tell them to take the time to listen to the music playing in their mind, and note whether they *like* what they are hearing. Internally, can they make every note a note that they *like* to play?

      iii. Once they are enjoying each note in their mind they are ready to put *feeling* into their playing.

      iv. The next step is fun and creative: have the class listen to the music in their head and, at the same time, think what they can do on the guitar to get others hearing what they are hearing.

      v. If the music is strong when visualized, students should show it in their playing. Have them give extra weight to the notes they feel most strongly about. They are now adding feeling. It takes time to develop this but it will help the students to become very interpretive in their playing.

   d. Mark any unusual observations in your grade book.

LESSON 6F: FORMAL ASSESSMENTS FOR LEVEL 6

1. Students will form into groups/ensembles with one person to a part. Each ensemble will select one of the following pieces to perform for the class. Use Worksheet #27 as an assessment tool, and distribute Worksheet #27a to the class so they can create peer assessments.

   "Minuet in G"

   "Aguado Study"

   "One Finger Blues"

   "Romanza"

   "Simple Gifts" (solo or duo)

2. Are the students able to perform their selected pieces while meeting the following criteria?

   a. Chord changes in tempo

   b. Accurate notes

   c. Appropriate picking patterns

   d. Appropriate blend

   e. Following dynamics and the musical road maps

   f. Develop feeling in the performances

3. Some suggestions:

   a. Look for opportunities to take the ensembles to the rest of the school or community.

      i. Lunch concerts

      ii. PTA meetings

      iii. Library concerts

      iv. Other humanities classes such as language or history

   b. Contact your local music store, and invite professional guitarists to play for the students and also give tips as the class performs in ensembles and solos in a "master class" format.

CLASSROOM MANAGEMENT AND ADVICE

Noodling: "Noodling" on the guitar (irresistible to anyone holding a guitar) can be very disruptive to any class. A good approach for controlling the impulse to noodle is to ask the students to place the guitars in their laps with the strings facing down. (Of course some inventive students will realize the back of the guitar makes a great drum.) This is a good "time out" classroom technique when providing instructions and gives you the authority to let the class know when it is time to play. You can also reference performing groups (orchestras, bands, recording artists, etc.) that do not accept unprofessional conduct to help reinforce that you expect the class to also follow this professional model. This is important to make sure students do not disturb others.

Guitar Straps: Using guitar straps is a great way to establish good technique even when seated. Both feet should be on the floor and the strap should be positioned to provide easy access to the neck of the guitar without strain or tension. The guitar should be tilted back slightly to let the back of the instrument vibrate, improving the projection of the instrument.

Picks: There is a wide variety of picks available at your local music store. You can save money by buying picks in gross. When starting out the traditional pick (or plectrum) style with a medium or heavy thickness is appropriate. A good tip is to put a rubber band around the top of the headstock to slip the pick under—always keep two there, especially because picks do occasionally fall to the floor while playing or into the guitar's sound hole. This will hold the pick without warping it as is the case when picks are slipped into the guitar strings. There are also inexpensive pick holders (with double-sided tape) that can be placed behind the headstock.

Portfolios: As the students complete research, worksheets, and supplemental materials, you can ask them to build a portfolio. Determine the type of binder or notebook to be used to organize the material. Pocket folders or three-ring notebooks for three-hole punched papers are excellent. Make sure:

- Each student has clearly labelled his or her notebook or binder

- The students know they are responsible for keeping all of their portfolio entries and also keeping them organized

- If possible, students can also include CDs or tapes of their performances

- Inform the students you will periodically review portfolios for completeness, and instruct them when to bring the portfolio to class.

- An in-class filing system where students can deposit and/or collect their work for their portfolio is also helpful. The best place to install this filing system is near the entrance of the classroom. Make sure it is clearly labeled with class periods and the names of every student.

Additional Advice: When developing a syllabus for the course, use the template provided by your department or administration with the following possible additions.

- The school is not responsible for the security of personal instruments. Each student's name should be clearly marked on the case and guitar. Any student with a locking case should use it.

- Office telephone number and e-mail of the instructor should be included.

- All cell phones, pagers, instant messaging, and other personal communication devices must be switched off during class.

- A warning that the schedule and procedures in the course are subject to change in the event of extenuating circumstances.

THE NATURE OF GUITAR TABLATURE

Tablature, or TAB, actually predates standard music notation. Tablature is an illustration of the specific fingerings to be played, while music notation is an illustration of the notes and rhythms to be performed. Tablature shows you what to play physically on the guitar; music notation tells you what you are playing musically. Tablature is shown as an additional staff that contains six lines representing the six strings of the guitar. Numbers representing frets are indicated on the strings.

Place your guitar on your lap. Now view Figures 1A and 1B to illustrate how tablature provides a graphic representation of the note locations on the neck. The bottom tablature line represents the 6th string; the top line depicts the 1st string. With tablature, numbers are placed on the TAB lines to illustrate frets. These fret numbers show where the notes indicated in the standard notation are located on the neck.

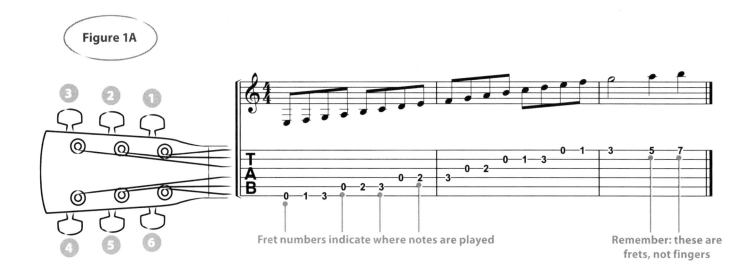

Figure 1A

Fret numbers indicate where notes are played

Remember: these are frets, not fingers

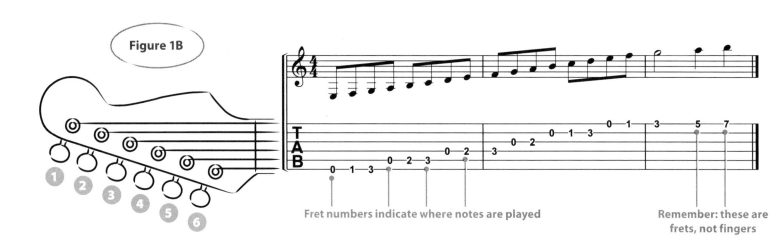

Figure 1B

Fret numbers indicate where notes are played

Remember: these are frets, not fingers

Since the guitar can have the exact same pitch on several different strings, tablature can be helpful to show the exact place on the guitar neck a note should be played. For example, the following G can be played in four different areas on the guitar—open position, 3rd string; 5th fret, 4th string; 10th fret, 5th string; and 15th fret, 6th string.

Figure 2

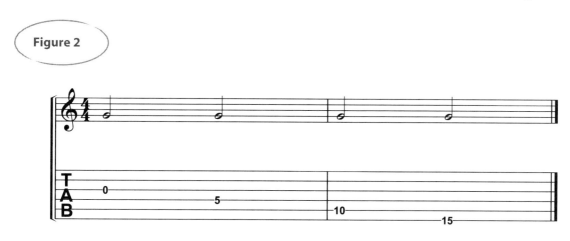

With tablature you can even have rhythm stems applied to the fret/string staff to illustrate the duration of the notes (see Figure 3). In this way it is possible to use only a tablature staff for the guitarist to perform a piece of music.

Figure 3

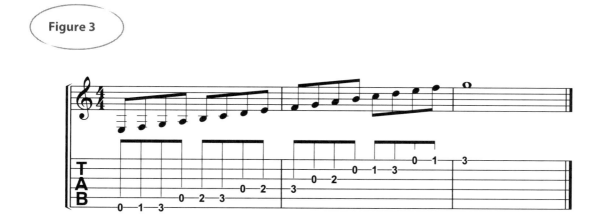

NATIONAL STANDARDS FOR THE ARTS

Federal funding was provided to form a set of voluntary national standards for education in basic core subjects as part of the Goals 2000: Educate America Act (1994). Through this initiative, music and the arts gained federal recognition for the first time as core subjects in public K–12 curricula. The goals entail nine content standards for music education. The developers recommended that students learn to comprehend, analyze, synthesize, and apply the following nine content standards:

NS1 (Singing) ....Sing, alone and with others, a varied repertoire of music

NS2 (Playing) ....Perform on instruments, alone and with others, a varied repertoire of music

NS3 (Improvising) ....Improvise melodies, variations, and accompaniments

NS4 (Composing) ....Compose and arrange music within specific guidelines

NS5 (Reading)...........................Read and notate music

NS6 (Listening).........................Listen to, analyze, and describe music

NS7 (Evaluating) ....Evaluate music and music performances

NS8 (Making Connections) ...Understand relationships between music, the other arts, and disciplines outside the arts

NS9 (History & Culture) ....Understand music in relation to history and culture

This key can be used to identify the abridged standards addressed within each lesson in the teacher edition.